ISRAEL AND THE CHURCH

Contribution to a Dialogue Vital for Peace

RESEARCH IN THEOLOGY
EDITED BY DIETRICH RITSCHL

ISRAEL
AND THE CHURCH

CONTRIBUTION TO A DIALOGUE VITAL FOR PEACE

Markus Barth

JOHN KNOX PRESS
Richmond, Virginia

Unless otherwise indicated, Scripture quotations are from the *Revised Standard Version of the Bible,* copyrighted 1946 and 1952.

Standard Book Number: 8042-0650-3
Library of Congress Catalog Card Number: 77-85426
© M. E. Bratcher 1969
Printed in the United States of America

INTRODUCTION

The appearance of Markus Barth's *Israel and the Church* is especially timely at a moment of renewed political tension in the Near East and of continuing passivity and misunderstanding among Christians in their position toward Israel.

The present volume is also appropriate as a part of *Research in Theology*. These books are designed to help meet the interests and needs of the scholarly theological community by providing a means of facilitating and accelerating the publication of original manuscripts which will fall into three categories:

(A) monographs containing a scholarly, technical apparatus,

(B) translations of recent or older foreign language material,

(C) vital theological contributions to contemporary issues— of which *Israel and the Church* is one.

DIETRICH RITSCHL

Pittsburgh, Pennsylvania
May, 1969

CONTENTS

DIALOGUE AND PEACE TODAY

A FOREWORD

————————————◆•◀◉▶•◆————————————

After the Six Days War of June, 1967, it appears difficult to resume a conversation between Jews and Christians about the deepest and highest things that challenge and worry, unite and divide them. Indeed, to continue this conversation today may prove more difficult than it was to start it.

Christians are accused of standing aloof and keeping silent when the very existence of the Israeli state and the survival of all its Jewish citizens were at stake. Was not the attitude of uncounted high- and low-ranking Catholics and Protestants exactly the same at the time of the Nazi horror? Even Jews who have never cared much for the observation of the Torah or for the goals of Zionism, today are requesting that all partners in a Jewish-Christian dialogue fully endorse the claim of the Jews upon the land that once was promised by God to Abraham and his children. Historically well-founded counterclaims and passionate complaints of the Arabs residing in Palestine, who for a long time have possessed and often skillfully cultivated the land, are met by references to the need for a Jewish homeland; the Balfour declaration; the division of Palestine by the United Nations; the foundation and successful defense of the state Israel; the right to military security and a unified capital. The land, *eretz Yisrael,* and the reunited city, *Yerushalaim* as praised by emotion-loaded new songs, have become much more than a place where Jews may live in security. The land and Jerusalem are now raised to the rank of a symbol. As such they have become a theological and humanitarian criterion. The concern for the land and the city has united orthodox and secularized Jews. No wonder that Christians are asked to understand and accept this fact before a basic dialogue can be reopened!

But the events of 1967 have so far produced a different reaction among many Christians. Certainly there are but few who fail to join in the joy over Israel's survival in a most critical situation and who would not admire her courage in facing the overwhelming power of her sworn enemies. Yet, the majority of the Christians are baffled by a new phenomenon: They have to learn that—since Israel's military victory—Jews all over the world feel inclined to regard Israel's blitzkrieg as a "holy war," similar to the ones fought by Joshua, Gideon, and David. Before this war the Christians' image of "the Jews" was based on their resemblance to the Suffering Servant of Isaiah. Now a new image has arisen: Jews of today identify themselves with their heroes of old and scorn the worn-out image which in our minds has linked them so closely with the one Jew to whom we owe salvation.

Christians are apprehensive also over the fact that, at least for the time being, the voices of those Jewish scholars and politicians in Israel are silenced who, following Martin Buber's views, sought for a wise solution to the problem of Israeli-Arab coexistence. Instead there are voices affirming that Auschwitz is as much overshadowed by the foundation of the Israeli state as death is by resurrection. Others declare Auschwitz an event of equal importance to the exodus, though Auschwitz reveals only God's hiddenness. The common denominator of these and other novel interpretations of Jewish history is the emergence of Israeli power. I have heard a Jewish scholar warning his fellow Jews of nothing less than triumphalism. Certainly the time has passed at which Christians (as it were, the sole possessors of power) could believe to have done the right thing merely by acknowledging their guilt in the pogroms stimulated or tolerated by the church, by pitying or admiring victims of anti-Semitism, or by a condescending recognition of the Jewish heritage inherent in Christian doctrine, ethics, organization. Just as the former monopoly of power is shattered in matters related to race, civil rights, socialist countries, developing nations, parent-child relationships, so it is in the case of Christians and Jews. Patronizing has revealed its internal weakness and corruption; it will no longer do. Inasmuch as mission was a concomitant of exporting one's riches or of colonialization, it has no future. All the more burning is the question posed to me by a militant professor of theology at the University of Jerusalem: Do you Christians love us less after we gained victory and power than you would have done if we had again, as in earlier times, been defeated and destroyed?

For both Jews and Christians the situation and the special problems posed by it are so new that everybody may be forced or inclined to prefer extensive private reflection and meditation to public confrontation and discussion. But the risk and cost of suspending all serious conversation are greater than all possible gains attributed to the humility and realism manifested by silence and factual separation. If Jews and Christians are brothers—and I hope to show that they are—they cannot stop caring for one another. They will ask questions, they will seek to understand, and occasionally they will not withhold suggestions or warnings. Above all, they will certainly not ask, What can I gain from an exchange with a brother? Rather they will acknowledge that they are plagued with so many seemingly insurmountable difficulties that they need more than anything else a cognate friend. If they believe in one God, the Creator, and if they hope for one Messiah to be manifested on earth, then neither Jews nor Christians can separate the discussion of heavenly and earthly, eternal and temporal things. No temporal event or decision or dissent can make them give up the hope that their brothers seek—as much as they do themselves—for faith and obedience, and that they act in good faith. Despite catastrophic experiences such as the occupation of Czechoslovakia by allied Socialist nations, Marxists and Christians will continue to meet at conference tables. Even Lyndon Johnson finally had to concede that discussion with Hanoi and the National Liberation Front might lead further than military escalation. Columbia's president met with Students for a Democratic

Society to find a way toward reforming the university. If this is the realism of worldly powers, what a shame if Jews and Christians cannot share their ultimate concerns! The spiritual, cultural, political, personal, and academic problems that beset them are so weighty and urgent that they need one another for a common quest, common labor, a common approach to solutions vital for all mankind. Otherwise, their mutual disregard and contempt demonstrate that they fail to believe what they assert regarding God's fatherhood over all, the brotherhood of men, the responsibility of the free. The *shalom* of God, which is for all the world, was and is still first experienced by the natural and spiritual children of Abraham; they have been chosen and equipped to attest to that peace in word and deed and common suffering. How could the members of God's people, whether born as Jews or joined to Israel from the nations, abdicate their election and primogeniture by stating that they cannot understand and cannot talk to one another? The peace they are given and for which they yearn is a light that will shine for every man.

The invitation and contribution to dialogue given on the following pages is not made on the basis of a vague trust that dialogue in itself will solve all problems. My intention is solely to come to grips with some of the burning issues. It may prove more hopeful to attack them than to drown in individual and mutual despair and give up all attempts for finding peace.

The three pieces contained in this little book have first been speeches, delivered in response to requests made for a theological discussion of the Jewish-Christian issue. The original speeches have been continually revised and augmented and sifted, until they were finally edited by my wife, Rose Marie. In order to retain some of the original character of these contributions to an ongoing discussion, references to learned books and more popular literature have been kept to a minimum. The questions regarding the Messiah, the discovery of the dramatic and ever new message of the Bible, the nature of obedient faith, and the basis of community and peace have certainly not been superseded or made immaterial by the Six Days War.

Jewish hearers of the original speeches have rightly observed that I am more critical of church thought and practice than of Jewish traditions. They asked me repeatedly whether I told these things to them only or also to groups composed of Christians only, and they wondered about the reaction I might find among Protestants and Catholics. The revised addresses are now republished for the purpose of preventing a frustration of the hope of the Jews.

MARKUS BARTH

Pittsburgh, Pennsylvania
December 3, 1968

I

WHAT CAN A JEW BELIEVE ABOUT JESUS—
AND STILL REMAIN A JEW?*

———◆•◄►•◆———

Belief in Jesus the Messiah cannot be advertised or sold, either as a package or in parts, to anyone, least of all to the Jews. Faith is not a composite or a given number of ingredients. No one is able to predict or delimit what changes even a grain of faith will effect. And a faith seemingly resplendent with personal assurance and universality can falter at the first opportunity. Neither Jesus himself nor any other Jewish teacher has shown the slightest intention to impose faith on anyone.

Reinhold Niebuhr and Paul Tillich[1] have denounced the imperialist attitude with which Christians have often engaged in "mission to the Jews." Niebuhr opposes the conversion of Jews to Christianity, because he wants to spare them any possible later guilt feelings for having endorsed the religion of the majority. Tillich sees no danger in the conversion of individual Jews. But he warns the Christians against aiming at any mass conversion of the Jews, because he attributes to Judaism a specific religious function in the Christian era. The main reason against the traditional mission to the Jews is, however, neither psychological nor speculative. The Holy Scriptures do not treat Israel as a nation (*goi*) like the others to whom the Christians must "go." But they describe Israel and its representative figures as God's own missionary to the nations. Gentile-

_____
* A lecture given on February 24, 1965, at a Brotherhood Dinner in the Tree of Life Synagogue, Pittsburgh, Pa. Formerly published in the *Journal of Ecumenical Studies,* Vol. 2, 1965, pp. 382-405. Used by permission.

born individuals should think twice before they presume to undertake the duty to "convert" to the one living God God's chosen witnesses. The New Testament does not deny that the Jews pray to the same God as the Christians. Even if we are children of Abraham in a special sense, we are yet subject to the same God and represented by the obedience of the same patriarch. At the time that Abraham was promised a son and heir, he was also assured that he would become father of many nations. His faith is set before the Romans and Galatians as the decisive type of the faith by which men are justified.

Rabbi Steven Schwarzschild is right, however, when he observes that I do "not really abandon the Christian desire to bring Israel to Jesus—no believing Christian could."[2] Of course I can only speak out of my own convictions, but it is precisely because of them that I have to respect fully the faith and conviction of the Jews. Therefore, I will not pressure them to betray the faith of the fathers. What is called for is witness given in dialogue rather than mission.

The specific questions which I will try to answer are all derived from the theme assigned to me by Rabbi Hailperin. They are these: Who is Jesus? Who is a Jew? What is faith? All these questions have a common denominator. We would like to know what truth is and how all of us may become true to it.

A. WHO IS JESUS?

The question "Who is Jesus?" is answered in the New Testament and by many Christians with various statements: He is the Messiah, the Son of the living God, the Savior of the world, the King of the Jews and as such the King of kings; he is the image or the Word of God; he is the bringer and ruler of the new aeon (the *olam habah*). All of these titles are taken from Israel's Bible and the Rabbinic and Apocalyptical tradition.[3] For Jews they are nothing new; only their exclusive attribution to one person in history, Jesus of Nazareth, is for them a surprise and a scandal. It is different with the so-called dogmas of the Christian church. Although they represent a development and elaboration of the biblical confessions, they not only are formulated in different languages (Greek and Latin) but also use images and concepts that are not found in the Hebrew Bible except perhaps in the Wisdom Literature. Creedal sentences set forth the terminology of incarnation, resurrection, human and divine natures of Jesus Christ, and the Trinity, and the mysteries of atonement, of the sacraments, and of the church (the body of Christ). All the respective dogmas could not have possibly been phrased in the language of the Torah, the Prophets, the Psalms, or the Mishna and Talmud. The new terminology of the early church's dogmas is not something external or only nominal. But because in God's history with Israel a new event of unique importance had taken place, new words had to be found for its proclamation. Little wonder, therefore, that Jews would react to these dogmas of the Christians with great suspicion. They may seem to the Jews more pagan than biblical.

But what do Jews themselves say about Jesus? In contradiction to slanders and attacks occasionally promoted during earlier periods, great Jewish scholars of recent times agree with less trained members of Jewish congregations in expressing deepest respect for Jesus. He is accepted as a teacher, a prophetic figure, and a martyr in the best of Jewish traditions; for there is almost complete harmony between his teachings in the Sermon on the Mount (Matt. 5-7) and the best of Rabbinical *halacha*. Also newer research in the nature and history of Pharisaism[4] has shown that despite clashes between Jesus and the Pharisees, a broad realm of common concern must not be denied. Today it is widely assumed in Jewish circles that supernatural attributes like Son of God, preexistence, omnipotence, sacramental presence were artificially tacked on the humble teacher of Nazareth after some of his disciples had gone through visionary experiences which moved them to the conviction that Jesus was exalted to the right hand of God and therefore was essentially equal to God. Thus Jesus, who according to the most ancient sources never called himself God, is said to have been deified in and by the belief of his followers. Among the outstanding initiators of this belief, John and Paul are singled

out. Though Jewish born, the author of the Fourth Gospel
and the great missionary to the Gentiles are considered to have
succumbed to the contemporary Hellenization of Judaism to
such a degree that they went to the limit or beyond the limit of
denying God's uniqueness and transcendence.

This does not mean that Jewish scholars judge as perverse
and syncretistic everything that John and Paul did and said for
the benefit of Gentiles. But there is a pronounced tendency to
hold that what is good in Paul's and John's teaching is of
Hebrew origin and what is not Jewish is no good. This, for
example, is the opinion of Leo Baeck and H. J. Schoeps.[5]

Among Protestant biblical scholars there is disagreement as
to whether Paul and John should be explained as Hellenists or
whether they should be understood on the line of "once a Jew,
always a Jew."[6] The movement toward understanding Paul
against his Hebrew background leads distinctly away from the
Tübingen image of Paul's place and role, which made him in
every aspect an alternative and antagonist to the supposedly
narrow-minded ceremonialist and legalist character of Judaism.[7]
In their own way, both Luther and Hegel were the fathers of
this view. And somewhere in the background looms Marcion,
the Gnostic.

But wherever traditional or more recent research leads, Jews
and Christians appear to have taken their positions: the Jews
against, the Christians in favor of, the belief in Jesus the Son
of God, the Messiah, the Savior, as he was proclaimed not only
by Paul and John but also, though in different ways, by the
other New Testament writers. In the course of his discussion
with Martin Buber, K. L. Schmidt once said, "Were the Church
more Christian than it is, the conflict with Judaism would be
sharper than it can be now. . . . We Christians must never tire of
keeping this one conflict alive."[8] Rabbi Steven Schwarzschild
certainly does not abate the issue when he asks, Why make so
much noise, e.g., at the Second Vatican Council, over the exe-
cution of one man by the Jews, two thousand years ago, when
in our time Christian nations of the West have exterminated
six million Jews?[9] Arguing on a different level, he told me once

bluntly, "What Christ is for you Christians, the Torah is for us Jews." He probably thought of the embodied will and presence of the living God. It looks as if there were hardly a possibility of understanding, not to speak of reconciliation, between Jews and Christians whenever the central question is squarely faced: "But who do you say that I am?" (Matt. 16:15).

Still, I would like to point out four things that might prevent our building between us an impenetrable wall:

1. The dogmas of the Christian churches should not be understood as propositions or definitions. Rather, they came into being and are meant to serve as pointers to something over which man has no control and which he cannot define. Just as the written and oral Torah has the function of pointing out (*yarah*) the way in which the Lord comes and the ways in which men are to walk, so also dogmas are signposts erected in times of conflict, doubt, and error to call Christians to respect the mystery of Jesus Christ and to submit to it. They are to guard his mystery against encroachments of physics or metaphysics, moralism, transcendentalism, magic superstitions or mythical abstractions. Every Jew knows that God is greater than the Torah and man's understanding of it. Equally Christians are reminded by their dogmas never to stop seeking and admiring Jesus Christ whom they would confess. Jesus Christ is much more than any dogma ever can spell out.

2. Early Christian teachers in Antioch (Syria) and Byzantium have held that historically Jesus was nothing but a man endowed by God with an abundant measure of the Holy Spirit. From the age of enlightenment up to modern times historical-critical New Testament scholars[10] have been of the opinion that, through an act of faith on the part of his disciples only, Jesus was elevated to the rank equal to God. The earlier and the later theories may differ in many respects. They agree, however, in the proposition that all that is said about Jesus Christ's divinity, whether in the Bible itself or in the church's dogmas, was only attributed to him and could not historically be proven as essential to his own self-understanding. The Christians endorsing this point of view seem basically to agree with many

Jews. They are certainly free from the suspicion of any polytheism. Their theory was called Adoptianism or Monarchian-
ism.

Adoptianism and various similar attempts to come to an
understanding of Jesus by serious consideration of his humanity
only, were opposed by the doctrine of those Christians who
would make light of, if not actually deny, his humanity. These
Docetists were not interested in Jesus' life on earth. They considered his human body and his death less as facts than as a
kind of appearance. By its negation of the incarnation, Doce-
tism obviously contradicts the New Testament proclamation of
the mystery of Christ just as much as does its Adoptianist coun-
terpart.

Some councils of the early church declared both of these
extreme theories heretical. They still are considered misleading
by all Christians who would believe the Prophets' and the
Apostles' testimony to the mystery of the Messiah. The dogmas
accepted in the fourth and fifth centuries under Alexandrian,
Roman, and Cappadocian leadership and reaffirmed by the
Eastern, the Roman Catholic, and the Protestant churches, did
not choose one of those easy ways of confining Jesus either to
the human or the heavenly realm. They all want to affirm,
each in its own way, that heaven and earth are joined together
in Jesus Christ because in him God and man are reconciled
and made one. But even the most venerable of the existing
confessions are subject to further discussion.

This ongoing quest and debate may show how stumbling,
imperfect, and ever-unfinished are the ways in which Christians
attempt to confess who Jesus is. If Jews wonder how Christians
dare to make any logical and unambiguous statement concerning the identity, mission, and function of Jesus of Nazareth,
all humble and honest Christians wonder with them. If Christians should ever try to manage Jesus Christ according to their
own ideas of what befits a Messiah, they would follow the disastrous example of the Apostles Peter and Judas, who both, on
different occasions, attempted to move their master in the direction of their own misinterpretation of his Messiahship. They
were rebuked and their efforts failed.

3. Jesus never called himself God; and according to Matthew and Luke,[11] he never clearly said, I am the Messiah. Rather, when he spoke of himself (in this, at least, the Gospels of Matthew, Mark and Luke agree), he preferred to use the cryptic title "Son of man." He predicted that his identity and function would be made public only when he would come again as the judge appointed by God. Thus he treated his Messiahship as something hidden that was to be revealed only after his death.[12] Now his disciples were convinced that by appearing after his resurrection, he had already fully disclosed to them (though "not to all the people," Acts 10:40-41) what was hidden before. On this basis they began to teach and preach among Jews and Gentiles about Jesus and the salvation wrought by him. But they did not forget that there was still another "coming" of Jesus to be expected: his return on the clouds, with angels, in the glory of God the Father.

This Second Coming is usually called the Parousia. In America, many members of great established denominations are hardly aware of this promise of Jesus; and if they are, they seem to care little about it, for it looks like an embarrassment to faith and ethics, like a piece of an antiquated, mythological world view which had better be left to California sectarians or Negro spirituals. But such an attitude is taken at great risk. For without the fulfillment of this promise of Jesus, his Messiahship is neither complete nor fully demonstrated and proven.

Or can there be another way to prove Jesus as the Messiah? We admit that since the beginning of the second century Christians have sought, compiled, and repeated quotations from the Torah, the Nebiim, and the Ketubim to "prove" to the Jews the Messiahship of Jesus, the superiority of grace over law, the excellence of universalism. But little good it did them or any Jews. Also Christians have engaged—and I am ashamed to mention it—in many other tactics (ranging from subtle bribe by a cup of soup to plain murder) to impose their faith upon the Jews. Again it was to no avail. They only loaded immeasurable guilt upon themselves and made the Jewish minority suspicious of any approach taken by the Christian majority. The New Testament does not yet know of any mission to the Jews carried

out by baptized Gentiles; Galatians 2:7-9 tells of an early for-
mal agreement according to which Jewish-born Christians
would bear this responsibility. Paul, the missionary of all missionaries, does not withhold his witness from synagogues and
Jerusalem, but he does not subsume Israel among the "nations"
or pagans to whom he has to preach.[13] Wisely he leaves it to
God to make the Jews jealous,[14] and to the day of resurrection
to bring salvation to "all Israel."[15]

In brief, the Messiahship of Jesus, of which Judaeo-Christians such as Peter and Paul are firmly convinced and which
in a more or less straightforward way is affirmed by Christians
of Gentile origin, is as yet finally and fully revealed neither to
Jews nor to Gentiles. All men are dependent upon the revelation yet to come. Christians as well as Jews depend on the future
coming and manifestation of him who is God's Messiah and
their common hope. Rather than being divided like possessors
and paupers or like soft-hearted and hard-hearted people,
Christians and Jews are united as fellows-in-waiting.

4. The concern which moves Christians, already before
Jesus' second coming and despite some outspoken protests from
Jewish quarters, to call Jesus God of God, Light of Light, Savior
of all men, and Head over all things, is not to deify a man.
Christians would indeed be idol makers and idolators, following
the suggestion of the serpent in the garden or the fateful
procedure of the king of Tyre (Ezek. 28), if they took such a
step. Rather their concern is doxological, i.e., to give praise to
God on the ground of his deeds and his self-revelation. Is God
only on high, far away, majestic in giving commands, bountiful
in making promises? Certainly an idealist's notion of a tran-
scendent being might drive men to embrace such a concept of
God! But the history called into being by God taught all men
a different lesson. He who is high proved free and willing also
to be low. He who walked in the garden by evening trod also
through mud. The same who commands knows also obedience.
The same who gives great promises gives himself to fulfill his
promise. God is not impassible. He suffers for Israel; he also
suffers from all the miseries that are caused and endured by all

mankind. He suffers not only in his heart but also here on earth, in this one fellowman, Jesus. Therefore, Christians are bound to confess that God was in Christ reconciling the inimical and estranged world to himself.

A Jewish philosopher once told me that the difference between a Jew and a Christian was this: "Your God is humble; we Jews cannot accept such humility of God." Indeed, what can be perceived in Jesus Christ, and what Christians want to praise, is this: God is high as well as low, not only far but also near, blessing with everything good, and carrying the brunt of rejection. Paul may still be right when he states that what baffles the Jews is not the so-called divinity but the cross of Christ (1 Cor. 1:23). When Christians confess that in Jesus there is more than Moses, more than Solomon, more than Isaiah, this "more" consists not of an addition of another God to the one God, nor of a substitute God as Marcion thought; it consists of the disclosure of God's humility—even the presence of God at the cross, where it seems that nothing but his absence was crying to heaven. That God was present and close precisely where he apparently was completely absent and hidden—this is what Christians would glorify.

The Gentile Christians, however, do not possess an easier approach to the cross of Jesus, and they cannot claim to understand its mystery better than the Jews. Gentiles no less than Jews are stupefied by this cross. No one has a way to explain or rationalize it. Everyone is too directly involved in both the guilt and the love, the defeat and the victory, manifested there. Instead of boasting of a theology of the cross, Christians may learn respect for the cross from Jews. Many Jews[16] are ready to take on the life and suffering of a haunted slave or a homeless refugee and to serve as mankind's scapegoat, which is hurried hither and thither and finally driven to its death. Even in early church interpretations of the most outstanding chapter about the servant of the Lord, Isaiah 53, there is an awareness that Israel might fulfill a redemptive ministry for the benefit of all mankind. In the New Testament, the followers of Jesus are urged to walk in their Lord's footsteps and gladly bear persecution as a despised minority.[17] But have the Christians, more than the Jews, borne the mark of the cross? Not all but many Jews have accepted dispersion (*galuth*) and defamation in a manner which shows greater and more costly faith than, for example, does the so-called theology of the cross which consists of words only. Christians should gratefully acknowledge what they can learn from faithful Jews about the suffering servant of the Lord and about patient cross-bearing. If Christians opened their eyes and hearts to the history of the Jews up to the present, they might realize that, beside the above-mentioned community of hope, there also exists a community of suffering between Christians and Jews. Unfortunately, it cannot be denied that Christians have outdone those Jews who above all seek a cheap peace with, and assimilation to, the culture of their environment.

Without listening to Israel's testimony to the Lord and without acknowledging God's continuing activity among the Jews, Christians cannot appeal to Jesus nor can they confess Jesus as God's Son and the Messiah. On the contrary, they may truly speak of God, who has revealed himself in Jesus and is present in him, only when they also recognize Israel as God's people and are learning from and with the Jews who is God's faithful servant. The message of the New Testament remains grounded in the testimony of the Old Testament. The New Testament by no means intends to characterize the Old Testament as antiquated or as an antithesis.[18] A passage like John 1:17, "For the law was given through Moses; grace and truth came through Jesus Christ," does not aim at setting up a sharp contrast between law and gospel. Emphasis is laid on the continuity of God's action. Through Moses God promised and commanded the mediation which in Jesus Christ became fact. The same God is at work here and there.

The wonder, amazement, joy provoked by Jesus made some men confess, "This is the Christ," "God is with him," "God is in Christ." Continuing in wonder is what makes a Christian.[19] Even when glory is given to God on behalf of Jesus Christ, it is not out of the presumption that God's mystery is now defined

and explained, but in abiding amazement: "Who then is this
. . . ?" (Mark 4:41). Neither Jews nor Gentiles, least of all
Christians, can stop asking this question.

B. WHO IS A JEW?

The topic suggests that "a Jew" and "what he can believe"
present a very specific problem. As a matter of fact, it has often
been supposed that a Jew, either because of his history or his
worship or the seemingly timeless character of Judaism, has
specific obligations and temptations, privileges and limitations
which are not shared by the rest of mankind. I have grave
reservations against this sort of distinction; it resembles all
too much an unhealthy segregationism which many Jews,
Christians, humanitarians, and forward-looking pioneers attempt to overcome even in our day. My reasons are the following:

1. From what I know about Jews through personal experience and literary study, they are not different from any other
seeking and erring, yearning and laboring, rejoicing and
grumbling, amazed or frightened human beings. To speak about
"the Jew," "a Jew," or worse, "the eternal Jew," means to make
use of a concept that belongs to mythology. This concept has
been known to produce anti-Semitism of one kind or another,
as has become evident not only in Hitler's or Rockwell's Nazism
but also in contemporary Soviet press polemics, not to speak
of the pogroms of medieval times. It is a startling fact that
any study of "the Jews," whether sociological or theological,
done by Gentiles or by Jews, by well-meaning or by ill-wishing
people, is prone to lead to further discrimination. In a conversation with some Jewish colleagues, I have been requested emphatically not even in sympathy to regard them as special in
any way, but simply as fellowmen. That Jews are men just like
all of us is an observation which involves the fact that they
differ strongly and radically among themselves.

As illustrations only from contemporary American phe-
nomena, there are Reform Jews, Conservative Jews, and

Orthodox Jews worshipping in distinctive synagogues. Mordecai Kaplan, Abraham Heschel, and the Williamsburg Hasidim
call for respect as Jews, each in their own right. Leon Uris'
Nazi-like *Blut und Boden* ideology is worlds apart from Herman
Wouk's affirmation of the role of tradition and rituals. Arthur
Cohen's openness for the cultural and philosophical problems
of Judaism in Germany since the time of enlightenment is
different from Will Herberg's sociological and theological approach to basic issues. R. L. Rubinstein's Freudianism may to
some extent resemble the professed atheism of an Israeli
journalist at whose side I was permitted to sit during a Seder
in a Conservative Jewish home, and yet they are of quite different characters. There are even Jewish anti-Semites and hap-
less Jewish victims who in concentration camps were forced to
cooperate with tormentors or murderers of innocent captives.
Basic differences also are found among the classic figures who,
during the past decades, were leading in the Jewish dialogue
with Christians. We mention only Franz Rosenzweig, Leo
Baeck, and Martin Buber.

It is a temptation for a non-Jew to despair of the confusion
and contradiction he finds even among his Jewish friends. But
despite all varieties of Jewish existence, it still is unique in its
kind. Not that the Jews could rightfully be called a race, a
nation, a culture-community, or a denomination like others.
Though here and there some common Jewish idiosyncrasies
may be detected and either admired or denounced, they do not
constitute this uniqueness. The only reasonable answer I have
found to the question, Who is a Jew? is this: He is a member of
the people whom God does not let go. Among all other peoples
on earth, God has chosen Israel to be his covenant partner;
and God does not break his covenant.

What the Scriptures say about Israel's election, preservation,
and judgment by God is noted with envy or hatred, with joy or
contempt. There is, however, no other description—even the
attempt of a most sympathetic definition—which could do
justice to Israel or Jewish existence as a whole. To make an
image of Israel proves no less possible than to make an image
of her Lord, because he cannot be left out of the picture. This

people has obeyed God and rebelled against him; it has confessed and denied him. It has suffered persecution and gloried
in the triumphs God gave it through his appointed servants.
Again and again this people has lost everything and yet has
made prodigious contributions to the advancement of mankind.
More afflicted than any other people, it also has been sustained in a marvelous and unique way.

The world's nations may develop according to the pattern of
rise and fall, but no such model applies to Israel. The Jews
live on as the people of God even in dispersion; the exile
(*galuth*) has never been only an ordeal but has always been
blessed with promise. Evidently all this reasoning does not make
sense unless God is given credit as the one who has shaped
and still warrants Israel's identity. Jewish identity is bound up
with the very identity of God and therefore can be discerned
only where God's faithfulness is believed. But whether he believes in it or not, a Jew remains addressed by God and equipped
to respond to him with obedience, suffering, and praise. "And
she . . . bore a son, and said, 'This time I will praise the LORD';
therefore she called his name Judah . . .'"[20]

Some Jews have tried to run away from their history and
calling. But the *epispasmos* (surgery applied to nullify the effect of circumcision) of the Hellenistic period, and the assimilation sought in all times of so-called "enlightenment," have not
prevented the nations from treating all Jews as belonging together. In a perverse way the common history and the belonging together of all Jews, whether orthodox or atheist, were
attested even by Hitler. By hating and destroying the Jews he
revealed his disdain for God's history with mankind, and he
attempted to obliterate the very essence of humanity, its dependence and reliance upon God.

Therefore the first answer to the question, Who is a Jew?
has to refer to the manifoldness as well as to the uniqueness
of Jewish existence and to the unerasable stamp left upon
earth by the specific history between God and this people and
between this people and the nations. There is no one sentence
or proposition by which a Jew as such can be defined. There is
only the possibility and necessity of telling his history. Jewish

existence can be studied only in the context of its long and unfinished history.

But a second answer must be added:

2. I know of one man whom I would dare call the Jew par excellence. His name is neither Moses nor Elijah, neither David nor Ezra, neither Nathanael (John 1:47) nor Paul of Tarsus, neither Hillel nor Maimonides nor any other great name in Israel, though each of these in his own way has many things in common with the man of whom I now must speak—Jesus of Nazareth.

There can be little doubt about his connection with Jewish history. Different genealogies delivered by the evangelists Matthew (ch. 1) and Luke (ch. 3)[21] agree in showing his rootage in Israel. His life was a summary and a representation of Israel's life. He was the living image of God, a light, an invitation, a sacrificial gift given by Israel to all mankind. His death, his resurrection, and the gospel of peace spread by his apostles have their seat and make sense only within the yet unended Jewish history. If Gentile-born Christians participate in any salvation at all, this salvation, preached and provided as it is by Jesus of Nazareth, "is from the Jews" (John 4:22).

What makes Jesus the typical and true Jew is not his self-consciousness. We know very little, if anything, of what he thought of himself, except that he knew in whom he was to confide and how he had to obey. He was certainly not a Narcissus enamored with himself, nor the leader of a movement set in motion to have himself elected, nor a desperado making capital of his self-hatred or self-pity. What distinguishes him among all Jews and all men is that he accepts God's judgment without reservations and limitations. He accepts man's condition, assumes man's guilt, faces God to intercede for friend and foe—and his offering is accepted. Moses had offered his own life to God for his people before Jesus did. Abraham pleaded even for Gentiles. The Talmud speaks of the merits of the fathers that are accredited to Israel; it also makes Abraham the patron saint of the pagan-born converts to Judaism. The great prophets were intercessors for Israel as much as the high priest was, especially on the Day of Atonement. The history of the Hebrews, past and present, is full of faithful martyrs. But Jesus' sacrifice was accepted by God in a unique and solemn way and vindicated before the Gentiles: Jesus was resurrected and exalted by God, and proclaimed Lord and Savior of mankind. He became the fulfiller of Israel's original mission: to be the showpiece and herald of God's blessing which overflows from Israel to the nations.[22]

Therefore, Christians are bound to affirm that Jesus is not just a Jew, but the Jew of Jews, the affirmation and culmination of Israel's history among and for the nations. Should anyone want to honor Jesus at the expense of Israel by presenting him as an alternative or substitute for the salvation which was to come from the Jews, he would disprove himself as a follower of Christ, the son of Mary. It is not a paradox, but fully in line with the many inspired leaders of Israel, that Jesus is not at once recognized by his own people, that he ushers in a dreadful crisis for his people, and that he refrains from giving proofs of his identity. For to be elected and beloved by God means to accept loneliness, chastisement, apparent failure, and to rely on the vindication of God, even the resurrection.

What does this exemplary Jew, Jesus, "believe of Jesus"? Certainly nothing that would prevent him from "remaining a Jew"! He believed in God, and his faith was inseparably linked with his faithfulness, his love, his obedience, his sacrifice. He did not withhold himself from service to the bitter end. Far from any denying and belying of his Judaism, precisely his attitude of total faith in God, total obedience to the law, total reliance upon the promises, made him a true Jew. Since, as we have already mentioned, he did not call himself "Christ," we might now go to an extreme and add that Jesus Christ was not a Christian—if this term means one who is separated from, or who attempts to be saved at the expense of, the Jews. Jesus was and remained a good Jew, the real Jew, accepted and glorified by God. This identity is the ground upon which he became and is called the "Savior of the world" (1 John 4:14).

3. When a Christian presumes to take up the question, Who or what is a Jew, he will have to answer, He is my brother! And he will have to add the qualifying statement, He is my senior

brother whom I have wronged and with whom I would be reconciled, if ever I am to enjoy peace with God. A parable told by Jesus (see Luke 15:11-32) may serve as an illustration:

A father had two sons. The younger asked for and received his share in the patrimony and left home to waste it with prostitutes. After he had lost all and had become so repulsive to every man that he was refused even the pigs' food, he remembered home and went home to confess his guilt before God and man and to ask for the lowest job. His father had been waiting for him and received him with outgoing love and joy. A great festival was celebrated for the returned prodigal. But the older brother, upon returning from a hard day's work in the field, would not join in the celebration. He remembered the contrast between his own labors and the vices in which his brother had engaged. The father had to go out to remind him of his undisputed privileges and to urge him to join the celebration arranged for the one who had been dead and had come alive again, was lost and found again.

One of the many possible meanings of this parable is the illustration of the relationship between Jews and repentant Gentiles. The priority and hard labor of Israel is as little disputed as the shameful life of the *goi* with the swine. Their history is different: The one has many things to be proud of; the other has absolutely nothing. The first is in a position to judge the other; the other has coming to him whatever humiliation and punishment may be in store. But the two are not left to themselves. God is the father of both, and thus they are and remain brothers. It is not the junior brother's right or mission to reproach his senior.[23] The father has reserved it to himself to call his older son to take part in the joy of his house together with the junior. This puts more than a damper or caveat upon traditional methods used by Christians to convert the Jews. Those who behaved like pigs and were saved from the swine can hardly go beyond confessing their guilt and showing fruits of repentance. It is certainly not theirs to prescribe to the Jews from an assumed position of superiority and security.

The parable may also serve to show that a Jew need not

become a *goi,* as little as the *goi* needs become a Jew, to enjoy
the privileges of the fatherly house. The unity which they
enjoy, because there is but one Father, is not streamlined or
uniform. As individuals remain individuals even when they are
"one in Christ" (Gal. 3:28, Col. 3:11; cf. 1 Cor. 12:12-13), so the
peoples' serving God does not deny, but upholds the special
history and character of its members, giving priority to the
common praise and mutual love of God over and across all
distinctions. If both have come to know that they are justified
by grace alone (cf. Gal. 2:15-21), then a Jew like Peter is free
on occasions to "live like a Gentile" and Gentiles, like the
Galatians, are free to become like Paul (Gal. 2:14, 4:12; cf.
1 Cor. 9:20-21). What Paul writes to emphasize unity and prevent schisms he does not write to bring about a uniform mass
of normal or neutral Christians who would not remember their
Jewish or Gentile origin, nor be aware of their salvation by
God's free grace. Just as Paul sometimes emphatically reminds
Judaeo-Christians of their Jewish past, so he does in a corresponding manner with Gentiles. The purpose of this differentiation is not to segregate the formerly Jewish from the formerly Gentile members of the church by stressing and defending
some inalienable values of each one's previous existence, but
to glorify the justification by grace and faith alone (e.g., Gal.
2:15 ff, 4:8 ff; Rom. 3:30). This means that the traditional
contest between Jews and Christians in matters of true worship,
absolute truth, or superior religion does not make any sense.[24]

Also the concomitant excitement over the question whether
there is any salvation outside the church or outside the synagogue may prove pointless. If Jews and Christians are brothers,
despite all errors, hypocrisies, crimes committed from either
side, and if Jesus the Jew is the one who brings to the Gentiles
the blessing promised to Abraham, then there is but one "house"
of salvation—God's. Then both Jews and Gentiles cannot be
children and servants of God without living together and listening to one another. When Gentile Christians denied Jews
brotherhood, respect, community, they despised and rejected
God's love. Neither for Christians nor for Jews is there love of
God without love of the neighbor. "On these two command-

ments depend all the law and the prophets," Jesus said (Matt. 22:40).

Christians have become wont to speak of "means of grace," and they have attributed to the Bible, preaching, the church, or the sacraments the dignity of being indispensable means of salvation. But the honorable function belonging to persons who become God's ministers for our salvation should not be transferred to things. Not the deployment and mystification of "means," but ever new acts of love and obedience are characteristic of God's children. The forgiveness granted by a fellowman becomes proof for the presence and forgiveness of God. It is a specific fellowman—the Jew—who is necessary for the *goi*'s salvation. For how can the returned prodigal enjoy peace in his father's house when the older brother does not rejoice with him? Even if the senior should only remind the junior of his sin and of his salvation by sheer grace, he renders him a necessary service.

In communion with Jews, Christians will be recipients rather than givers. Paul Tillich probably is right when he notes that people of Gentile origin need the testimony rendered by the Jews, lest they slip back into Gentile ways.[25] For this reason Jews have to be beseeched to participate in the innumerable attempts made by Catholics, Protestants, and Orthodox to recover now the unity of God's people on earth. If Jews were definitely excluded from the respective encounters, discussions, and decisions, the unity reached might well resemble a pagan symposium, but hardly the community of God's one people gathered from all the nations. Christians cannot help but beg the Jews to join the ecumenical movement, not for the sake of a super-church, but for the search of true knowledge, genuine service, and unity in love and reverence for the one God.

C. WHAT IS FAITH?

Are the Christians based on the same ground as the Jews and can they be sure they understand what they are talking about when they presume to speak about the faith of the Jews and to give their opinion about what a Jew can believe?

Even if one should like to answer this question positively, it is not certain that he has a right to do so. For the concept, meaning, evaluation of faith has a long history,[26] which at this place cannot be retold, dramatic and instructive though it be. Three aspects only will be singled out.

1. A believer in a caricature of both the Jews' heritage and the apostle Paul's message may be inclined to assert that faith is what Christians have and Jews lack. This notion, which unfortunately is widespread, seems to have originated from such statements as, "Israel who pursued the righteousness which is based on law did not succeed in fulfilling that law. Why? Because they did not pursue it through faith, but as if it were based on works."[27] An oversimplifying exploitation of this passage and similar New Testament texts makes all Jews people who boast of their election and privileged position before God; who believe, as did the heretical Pelagians, in salvation by good works; who contest God's right to judge them by assuming that their merits tie God's hands; who finally spoil genuine ethical behavior by their selfish speculation on a promised reward.

It is not entirely impossible (though not sufficiently proven) that before his conversion Paul himself held such beliefs—the third chapter of his epistle to the Philippians points in this direction. Perhaps many diaspora Jews understood the Law in a similar way.[28] Protestants like to blame Ezra and Nehemiah for leading Israel toward an "absolutization of the Law" and a concomitant legalism.[29] It appears certain that in and outside Jerusalem early Christian congregations were pestered by individuals and groups who wanted to be good Jews, and to glorify the Law of the Jews, by requesting Gentiles to add to their faith in Christ subservience to the Law or at least to some ceremonial observances.[30] Beside passages which praise God for the righteousness he accords men by his grace, the documents of the Qumran community include statements that have a ring of work-righteousness. In Galatia Paul had to oppose people who appealed to the Jewish law and tried to force on Gentile Christians certain legalistic prescriptions which they held to be absolutely necessary for salvation.

All this does not prove that a Jew who is true to Mosaic,

Prophetic, or Rabbinic tradition knows only of law and works and has no idea of faith. In Jewish teaching it is considered not a paradox but a tautology when it is said "[Abraham] believed the LORD; and he reckoned it to him as righteousness," *and* "Abraham obeyed my voice and kept my charge, my commandments, my statutes, and my laws" (Gen. 15:6, 26:5). What Habakkuk (2:4) writes about the life of the righteous in virtue of faith was understood in the traditional Hebrew text as life in virtue of fulfillment of the Law. But in the earliest Greek translation, the Septuagint, this text was interpreted as saying, "The righteous shall live by the faithfulness of God." The Qumran commentary on this passage speaks of faith in the Teacher of Righteousness. Not only Paul but equally the Talmud places greatest emphasis upon the indivisibility of faith and obedience. In various Talmudic contexts Exodus 14:31 and Micah 6:8 are quoted: "they believed in the LORD and in his servant Moses," and "He has showed you, O man, what is good; and what does the LORD require of you but to do justice, and to love kindness, and to walk humbly with your God?"

Therefore, a possessive or patronizing attitude does not befit Christians when the question of faith is discussed with Jews. Complete trust, sincere devotion, obedience until death, mystic introversion, and outgoing social commitment—but above all, reliance on and adherence to the revealed word of God—may be found at least as frequently among Jews as among Christians. The well-known statues of the Strassburg cathedral, representing the church by a rather proud and punitive-looking young lady and the synagogue by a humiliated, blindfolded girl holding a broken staff in one hand and a tablet (of the law) in the other, may be expressive of a medieval interpretation of 2 Corinthians 3. In this chapter Paul treats Israel's inability to see the glory of the Lord. But I agree with Franz Rosenzweig's and Martin Buber's[31] moving words on the figure of the synagogue. It shows forth Israel's suffering and her acceptance of God's judgment as gracious even though it is hard. It appears to me that even the medieval artist, his submission to official church teaching notwithstanding, put his love in the lady with the broken staff. She who reminds us of the Jewish girl, Mary, the Lord's handmaiden, and not her victorious competitor, is his masterpiece. She also is a better symbol of the true church. In this as in other cases Christians may learn from the synagogue what it means to be God's people. When Jesus said, "not even in Israel have I found such faith" (like that of a Gentile centurion, Matt. 8:10), he did not exclude the possibility that on other occasions Gentiles might wonder at the faith of the Israelites.

Still there is a remaining difference: Christians cannot and will not let go of identifying true faith with the faith of Jesus Christ and in Jesus Christ.[32] When with Paul they speak of justification by faith, they do not intend to substitute faith for other human works or attitudes. But they wish to confess that their sin is forgiven and their life is renewed by the grace of Jesus Christ alone. More specifically they mean by faith that fulfillment of promise and command and that communion of Jews and Gentiles with God which have been brought about by Jesus the Messiah. His birth from a lowly woman of Judah, his servant ministry leading him to the cross, his vindication by the resurrection, and his exaltation as King of the Universe —all these events are essential to the Christians' faith. Therefore, not only Jesus but also faith is understood by them in Messianic terms. God's Spirit, promised for the last days, makes Jesus the Messiah and gives faith to both Jews and Gentiles. This content and essence of faith—the very presence and triumph of God in Jesus and in the community of Jews and Gentiles assembled to serve him together—marks the distinction between Jews and Christians. The distinction may be deeply regretted by either side, but it cannot be denied. Jews and Christians still have to live with it. While Christians are already celebrating the Messiah who has come, Jews are still awaiting his coming. However, as has been said above, in some sense Christians are waiting, too.

Since God alone, and neither Jew nor Christian, is the criterion and judge concerning who truly believes in the Messiah, a mutual excommunication of Jews and Gentile Christians from the communion with the true Messiah does not make any sense. Christians should acknowledge that every Jew who with a burning heart yearns for the Messiah to come unconsciously but implicitly believes in Jesus;[33] even more, they should admit that their own understanding of the gospel, their own discipleship, their own faith and obedience to God who reveals and presents himself in the Messiah Jesus, are so fragmentary, stumbling, imperfect that they cannot set themselves up as a radiant example of how to believe. What real faith in the Messiah is, and in how far it is infinitely greater than the faith in Moses mentioned in Exodus 14:31 or than the faith in the Teacher of Righteousness (mentioned in the Pesher to Habakkuk of Qumran), is still to be learned by all men. Faith is not a ready-made vehicle into which this or that content may be fitted with some success. Neither is faith a mold or cast into which each man must be poured. Faith is the gift of grateful response to God's faithfulness as it is displayed in past and present manifestations. God creates faith, God judges faith—he who causes the last to be first. There is no uniformity of true faith, except that it will be faith in God. Peter was praying for all men when he said, "Increase our faith!" (Luke 17:5). The prayer, "I believe; help my unbelief," is the only appropriate prayer for those acknowledging that "All things are possible to him who believes" (Mark 9:23-24).

For these reasons Christians cannot claim against Jews to be the sole possessors and beneficiaries of true faith.

We proceed now to a second way of describing faith in the framework of Judaeo-Christian dialogue:

2. Many Jewish and Christian writers dealing with the problem of faith start from the observation that both Jews and Christians live by faith. But they speak of "two types of faith."[34] Among others the following differentiations have been made: Jewish faith is communal; Christian faith is individual. The first is earthly and concrete; the second, abstract and world-denying. One faces outward; the other inward. One accepts suffering; the other strives for bliss and success. Also action and conviction, ethics and dogmatics, being and becoming, have been juxta-

posed. Whenever such distinctions are made, a way is sought to affirm that both are true and precious, and both have their mystery—Judaism and Christianity. The intent is to show that while Jews and Christians may not worship and live in the same house, they yet form two houses that need each other for encouragement and conviction. This "two-house theory" might be compared to the complementary approach science offers to describe a substance on the basis of the quantum theory. Just as physicists may have to speak now of waves, now of particles, while they still have the same object in mind, so also Jews and Christians may perhaps serve as a living example for the fact that the mystery of God and of faith may only be approached in a dialectical way.

In conversation or dialogue, dialectics are to be given preference over simple propositions and definitions because they call for respect of the partner and for a certain self-limitation. Which wise man would not prefer Plato's dialogues to Aristotle's treatises, and the Talmud's kaleidoscopic way of instruction to the overassurance of some Protestant and Catholic interpretations of the Bible? But since God is God in person and not some kind of substance which may lend itself to scientific scrutiny; since he is the living Creator, Father, and Redeemer to whom glory, laud, and honor is due; and since he is not a mere topic or idea which may be analyzed or synthesized and upon which we may philosophize, the analogies just used in defense of the two-house theory prove nothing. Tensions between types of faith and contradictions of doctrine, worship, morals can be observed to run diametrically through Judaism as well as through Christianity. The same could be said about Marxism. Should one concentrate upon the above-named alternatives or complementary poles, he would by no means find all Jews assembled on one side, all Christians on the other. Very often a Jew and a Christian, perhaps also a Marxist, will understand each other better and find that they have more in common than the Jews or the Christians who meet each other as fellow-members of their respective communities. The tensions between individualism and collectivism, activism and quietism, objectiv-

ism and subjectivism, being and becoming, are historical in-
cidentals which perhaps represent a hereditary trait of Western
culture. They certainly are not essentials to the knowledge and
service of God. Perhaps they are or will be present in each man,
Western, Asiatic, or African. Paul the Apostle also reflects them
in his life and his message. But he does not absolutize them.

Or is Paul the man who invented, took over, or concocted
the supposedly Greek concept of personal faith? It is to be
noted that when he wants to explain what he means by that
faith through which we are justified, he quotes the Torah and
the Prophets. In short, he explains *pistis* by speaking of *emunah*.
Also he uses a Bible and employs a Greek diction which long
before had been utilized by the "seventy" translators and by
writers of Wisdom Books in the attempt to fulfill Israel's mission among the nations. For this reason I see little if any value
in the two-house theory. Jews and Christians live in one house
—God's.

The most far-reaching and penetrating distinction and coordination of Jewish and Christian faith, first made by Maimonides, was taken up by Salomon Formstecher in 1841 and forcefully defended by Franz Rosenzweig.[35] It holds that the teaching of the Nazarene and the mission carried out by the church
is good for the Gentiles, for it spreads truth over the world,
prepares the way for the Messiah, carries out the Jewish world
mission, serves to lead the nations of the world to the Father.
This understanding of Jesus and the church has a great ad-
vantage compared to the complementary analyses of Jewish
and Christian "faith" mentioned before. It understands the
faith of Christians in terms of a mission which is carried out
in God's name and for his praise. It does not seem to lack a
trace of envy, for Christians have attempted and accomplished
what was to be done by Jews. At any rate, here the history of
mankind is illuminated not by elaboration upon psychological,
ideological, or sociological human traits (i.e., not on the basis
of anthropology) but by pointing to its purpose, or omega
point: the glorification of God by all men as it is promised, for
example, in Isaiah 2:2-4 and Zechariah 14:9, 16.

But an element of condescension and self-excuse appears to mar the picture. While the Christians are not begrudged their success among the pagan masses and while the actual approach of the *goiim* to the living God is hailed, the Jews appear to recline in their seats and feel excused from taking a stand for or against Jesus. While they "believe about Jesus" that he is good enough for the Gentiles, leaving to his disciples the work they might have done, they appear to neglect their own search for truth and not to give God that honor which he deserves, nor their Christian brothers that support which they need. Truth brings obligations. If there is any truth in faith, if there is anything Messianic in Jesus, this will unite Jews and Christians much more closely than this last and most dynamic "complementary" theory does.

Therefore, we still have to ask again, What is Faith?

3. Many of the Western discussions about the nature of faith have been thriving upon the opposition or juxtaposition of faith and evidence, faith and reason, faith and life, faith and works, faith and doubt. The weakness of such explanations and comparisons is obvious: They fail to do justice to the fact that in the Bible perfidy, treason, and instability are the basic and most frequent opposites of faith. The traditional Western distinctions of faith from reason or from life or from doubt banish faith into the realm of epistemology: They make it appear to be a mode of intuition, cognition, or conviction, or a result of ideas and principles held fast; they lead into unending and fruitless debates and dilemmas characteristic of issues wrongly posed. Actually faith is not restricted to what occurs in the brain, the soul, the conscience of man. The root of the biblical (Old Testament) concept of faith, *emunah*, denotes a firm stand on solid ground. It means to correspond to God's covenanted faithfulness in a faithfully conducted life. Several prophets use the relationship of a beloved wife to her husband as an illustration and application of faith. Faith in God as well as knowledge of God has been called having God for a husband.

To use a different analogy, we can say that faith is citizenship in the realm where God is king. No citizenship exists only in relation to the head of a state; by definition it means fellow citizenship. The loyalty of a citizen shows in his behavior toward the members of the community and toward strangers. By entering the houses of tax collectors and Pharisees, by bringing sinners and saints together at one table, by dying for his people and for the many nations, and by inviting all of them together to share in a covenant meal, Jesus revealed and established the character of both God's kingship and man's citizenship. Faith, described in terms of the Gospels and Epistles of the New Testament, is to accept God's invitation with joy and to extend it to all. Faith is to behave all day long every day as one of the many partners in the covenant of love.

This description of faith may seem lacking in subtlety and possessing too many this-worldly, if not materialist, features. Be it so! For at least it corresponds to the insights and hopes of Moses, the Prophets, and the Psalmists concerning the coming, the recognition, the fruition, and enjoyment of God's kingdom. Nothing less than a Messianic banquet became the imagery of the time of fulfillment!

This means for us Christians that we cannot have faith and at the same time discriminate against those called by God before and with us. God has invited us through a Jew, Jesus. His call has brought us together with Jews. Jesus broke down the wall that divided us—including the wall that included some and excluded others. He brought both of us into one and the same house. He presides at a table and provides for both of us.

We Christians cannot confess our faith except by saying that Jesus joined the Gentiles to Israel; salvation is from the Jews. The Jews, for their part, know that to have faith in God means to rejoice in God's kingship over all nations. The Holy Scriptures remind them that Melchizedek and Zadok, Enoch and Cyrus, Ruth and Job and the Ninevites—those believing Gentiles—were joined to their history. For Jews and Christians alike, it is a matter of course that nobody can be a child and servant of God without becoming a brother and a fellow-servant in God's house. For both of them faith means to live within the community and unity of God's people.

Faith cannot stand separation, conceit, lack of love. Especially in the Pauline letters it is made very clear that the overcoming of the separation between Jews and Gentiles is the key to the removal of all dividing walls, whether they exist between races, nations, social classes, or age groups.[36] Where there is faith, no such wall will be considered as final.

Such faith only God can give. And we need this gift anew every day. We may talk about it at length, and certainly we are to do all we can to remove obstacles in its way or falsifications of its essence. But ultimately we can only pray for it—in prayers offered by each one in his place and in common prayer. When faith begins to mean that we are true to God, to his manifest will and his gifts, then Jews and Christians shall also be true to one another, as is fitting for brothers having the same Father.

II

WAS PAUL AN ANTI-SEMITE?*

In several oral discussions Jewish friends of mine have stated their attitudes toward Jesus and Paul in a way that can be summarized in the words, "Jesus of Nazareth was all right; he represented the best in Judaism, and Jews can learn many things from him. But when Paul of Tarsus became an apostle, there was trouble. It was his teaching and his work that separated the church and the synagogue in that fateful way which has led to ever new outbreaks of anti-Semitism among the nations."

The opinion and judgment expressed in these sentences are widely spread among contemporary Jews. Martin Buber, Joseph Klausner, Sholem Asch, H. J. Schoeps, and many others have not labored in vain. The time is over in which Jewish scholars sought to ward off claims and attacks of Christian missionaries by defaming or ridiculing the person of Jesus of Nazareth. But signs of painful surprise, if not regret, resentment, or outright hostility, are still found in Jewish studies of Paul's theology. Today certainly both Christians and Jews often are found in agreement when it comes to an evaluation of Judas Iscariot's betrayal and of Jesus' condemnation by a Sanhedrin controlled by the Sadducees. But although many Jews consider these acts a mark of disgrace in their history, they yet regard as equal infamy what they call Paul's apostasy from his own people.

* A lecture delivered at Temple Israel Meeting House in Boston, April 5, 1967. Revised reprint from the *Journal of Ecumenical Studies*, Vol. 5, 1968, pp. 78-104. Used by permission.

Since *Maimonides* there always have been Jews holding the irenic opinion that Paul's (and some other Christians') missionary efforts have borne some good fruits. Still it is not forgotten that Paul has supposedly disgraced his heritage.

In the following I want to discuss the causes which have led to such an understanding of Paul, to point out the situation which we therefore have to face in the Jewish-Christian dialogue, and to seek a way to break down the frozen fronts of our conversation. I do not intend to describe or criticize the image of Paul that has emerged in Jewish literature, accentuated here and there with friendly and unfriendly remarks. The heart of the trouble seems to lie in the way in which we Christians have understood or misunderstood Paul, rather than in Paul himself or in his possible misinterpretation by Jews. Therefore, I have to address primarily the Christians and among them, my fellow Protestants. May the Jewish readers show patience and magnanimity. It may well be that in this situation they will feel better understood and more adequately addressed than would be the case in direct confrontation or by immediate appeals—which almost necessarily would have to be taken for some kind of apologetic or rehash of former attempts at conversion.

What if Christian anti-Semitism, experienced a thousand-fold by Jews of all centuries, should have its roots in an age-old Gentile-Christian negligence and misinterpretation of Paul's message and work?

In order to answer this question, we shall first list and evaluate briefly such elements in the history of Paulinism or Christian exposition of Paul that have made him suspect of an anti-Semitic tendency. We shall then proceed to name a series of preconditions which, if met by Paul himself, would actually prove that his theology is anti-Semitic. We shall conclude by pointing out some features or tentative results of recent research which show not only the absence of sufficient evidence for a hidden or plain anti-Semitism in Paul, but even more the presence of the need for a drastic change in the attitude of Christians toward Jews. At the time of year when Jewish families clean their houses of old leaven, Christians, for their part, might follow Paul's admonition in 1 Corinthians 5:7-8 and do their share of housecleaning!

A. CAUSES FOR SUSPICION

1. The epistles of Paul and the traditions gathered in the Acts of the Apostles leave no doubt about clashes between Paul on the one hand, and diaspora and Jerusalem Jews on the other. An accusation similar to that raised against Stephen, the first martyr, was leveled against the Apostle Paul: "Men of Israel, help! This is the man who is teaching men everywhere against the [chosen] people and the law and this place [the temple]" (Acts 21:28; cf. 6:13-14). The question Paul raises in Romans 3:31, "Do we then overthrow the law by this faith?" is probably not just a rhetorical device, but a reflection of a Jewish reproach. In the early days of the church, things were not left at complaints and accusations; punishments, lynchings, and various persecutions took place. Although the reports found in Acts may contain some legendary or traditional stylistic elements (e.g., Acts 9:23 ff.), Paul's own statements (e.g., Gal. 4:29; 2 Cor. 11: 24-25) leave no doubt: As Paul himself, before his conversion, persecuted and "destroyed" Christians (Gal. 1:13, 24), so he, after his conversion, suffered persecution at the hands of the Jews.

Not all diaspora Jews wanted Paul penalized, and not all members of the Sanhedrin stood against him. Some of the former became Christians; among the latter, the Pharisees sided at times with Paul against the Sadducees. Still, Paul apparently never got a chance to receive in an orderly Jewish court all the benefits of due process of law. The fact that the Roman tribunals to which he was turned over protected him could hardly endear him to his Jewish opponents.

No indication is found, either in the existent New Testament records or in contemporary literature, that Paul, after becoming an apostle of Jesus Christ, ever harassed or harmed any Jews. The fact that he could not avoid opposition, persecution, or posthumous condemnation does not prove that he himself maligned his adversaries by prejudice, lies, or outright violence. If he was an anti-Semite at all, then his anti-Semitism was much more subtle.

2. It cannot be denied that the way in which Paul interpreted Israel's Holy Writings often brought him into conflict with the biblical exegesis and the oral tradition fostered by the professional lawyer-theologians and the conservative religious party of his time, the Scribes and Pharisees. What this man of the Spirit heard the Scriptures say, and the liberties he took in his association with Gentiles, were often distinct from contemporary Palestinian and Alexandrian interpretation and application. It looked as if Paul was throwing overboard the ceremonial traditions and the moral prescriptions of God's law and actually was treading underfoot the preeminence of the temple and the prerogative of Israel's election. Later Christian theologians, especially Origen, Augustine, the Medieval scholastics (except the school of the Victorines), pitted Paul's spiritual interpretation of the Scriptures against the literal, historical, fleshly interpretation of "the Jews."

In Reformation theology it was denied that any tradition, whether Rabbinic, Christian-Patristic, or Medieval, could compete with the testimony given "by the Bible alone." The Reformers equally opposed Jewish and Roman Catholic hermeneutical practices. Not a second source of revelation, and certainly not tradition alone, but the Scripture itself was to elucidate the Scripture. *Scriptura Scripturae interpres!* The testimony of the Spirit was held to be sufficient for true interpretation. Hebrew was gladly learned from Jewish scholars in order to approach the *"veritas Hebraica,"* and it was maintained (at least in theory) that there was no difference between literal and truly spiritual exegesis. The literal meaning demonstrated the truth; allegorical interpretation was discredited. Since according to Origen and others literal interpretation was characteristic of the Jewish reading of the Bible, the Reformers seemed to be open for some association with Jewish exegesis. Actually, however, they upheld the traditional demarcation lines. They did not yet know how closely Pauline hermeneutics was related to the methods employed, and to some results achieved, by the Qumran

community, by Philo or the Targums, by Mishnaic and Talmudic exegesis.

In brief, in the name of Paul (especially on the grounds of
2 Corinthians 3 and 5, as well as in the name of John) the
claim was raised that Protestants had a superior way of reading
the Scriptures. This claim is a variation but still an element of
the age-old Christian superiority complex which not only borders
on spiritual anti-Semitism but by necessity creates and sustains it.

3. Paul called Jesus Christ "Son of God" and he described
his personality and his acts by using predicates that formerly
in Jewish circles were attributed to God's preexistent wisdom,
the second Adam, the coming Judge of the universe, the apocalyptic Son of man, and the suffering servant of the Lord. Such
glorifying descriptions of Jesus Christ's origin, work, and ministry were also given by theologians of the second century
(Justin Martyr, Irenaeus, Origen). They were then combined with similar statements of the New Testament and finally
condensed in the formulation which declared Jesus Christ a
"second God," or "another God." How else but with horror and
protest could any Jew who prayed the *Schema Israel* (Deut.
6:4 ff.) react to such a blasphemy? Granted, the Ecumenical
Councils of Nicea, Constantinople, Ephesus, and Chalcedon
avoided the above-mentioned offensive diction, yet they formulated dogmas about the Trinity and the two natures of Jesus
Christ which for Jewish ears must have a ring of scandalous
polytheism. Inasmuch as these formulations seemed to drag
God down to a human or material level, or to ascribe to a man
equality with God, they sounded blasphemous to the Jews.
Since the church claimed to act on the basis of the Pauline
epistles, Jews were practically forced to assume that Paul himself had rejected the worship of the one God and Creator. Although in Paul's theological teaching hardly any trace of a testimony can be discovered that would contradict Israel's monotheism, Paul was considered as the one who in his Christology had
sown the seed of idolatry.

Actually there are quite a few Trinitarian formulations to
be found in Paul's epistles. His preaching on the incarnation,

crucifixion, and exaltation of Jesus owes much of its power to the fact that it treats of the eternal Son, Image, and Word of God. Nevertheless, the "orthodox" formulations of the fourth and fifth century are not simply consonant with those used by Paul. The church acted on her own responsibility when she used a terminology appropriate to the needs of post-apostolic periods. Has she, then, denied Paul's faith in the one and only God? The Councils of the Church repeated or expressed in their own words what to the best of their conscience they heard the Scriptures say. They formulated their confessions not in opposition to Jewish faith but in dialogue with Monarchianist, Arian, Aristotelian, or Monophysite concepts current in Antioch and Constantinople, in Alexandria and Ephesus respectively. Gentile Christian heretics, not the Jewish monotheism of the disciples of Moses, were opposed by the Councils. It is indeed possible and probable that, at an early stage of the intra-Christian controversies, the reluctance of the Antiochians to go along with that type of Alexandrian Christology that was later to prevail had something to do with the proximity of Antioch to the Jewish schools of Jamnia and Tiberias. Antiochian theology as well as the early pneuma-Christology of Asia Minor contained elements that had a less scandalizing effect on Jews than did the high Christology of Alexandria. Alexandrian theologians adopted exegetical methods and creedal formulations of Philo, the Jewish philosopher; but they pronounced their faith without taking into consideration a possible misunderstanding on the part of the Jews. When the Antiochian theology was defeated in the literary debates and in the power struggles of the Councils, it became much harder if not impossible for orthodox Jews to understand that the Church meant to confess before the nations the same faith as confessed by Abraham, Moses, and David. If a Christology like that of Paul from Samosata had found ecumenical approval, perhaps it might have been seriously discussed if not tolerated among Jewish theologians, for many another Messianic movement and speculation has been tolerated inside Judaism. Rabbi Akiba who praised Bar Kochba as the promised Messiah, as well as other erudite and pious admirers of other Messianic aspirants, remained respected teachers inside Judaism.

At any rate, the potential and actual harm done to those who keep the faith in the one God of Abraham, Isaac, and Jacob has to be attributed to the Patristic interpretation of the New Testament which resulted in the Nicean and Chalcedonian dogmas rather than to Paul himself. But it must also be stated that in their own way the Orthodox Fathers sought to ward off polytheism, anthropocentrism, and philosophical distortions just as vigorously as orthodox Rabbis have done at all times. They rejected the Gnostic notion of a God and Father of Jesus the Messiah other than the same God who had created heaven and earth and given Israel the law.

4. During the Second Vatican Council many people became shamefully aware that for centuries Christian liturgies, dramas, and theological writings have contained references to the "perfidious Jews," and have labeled the Jews as "deicides." Because Paul is the first theologian to have focused his teaching and preaching upon the passion and death of Jesus Christ, he appears to be the spiritual father of all the meanness and injustice done to the Jews in word and in deed, especially during and after the annual celebration of Lent. It would certainly not be fair if Christians tried to excuse themselves by making reference to the curse of the *Minim* that at various periods of Jewish history was pronounced with and without the words of the *Shmone Esre*. The evil done here and there is by no means equal. Since the Christians surpassed the Jews on the field of missions and since from the fourth century onward they could count on the assistance of Roman and Byzantine emperors, they were enabled to harm the Jews in a way and to a measure that cannot be compared to the curses murmured against the Christians in Jewish synagogues. It looked as if the Christians' hostile attitude toward all Jews was not only a cultural phenomenon of the growing church, but an essential feature of their faith. Otherwise, how could they dare to approach God in prayer and study the Scriptures—having curse words on their lips and Jewish blood on their hands?

But again, these results of spiritual conceit and scandalous intolerance are no proof that Paul himself instigated or fostered such behavior.

5. After Augustine had rediscovered for his time the rele-

vance and stringency of Paul's theology, the Augustinian monk Luther rediscovered Paul a second time. In his renewal and expansion of Augustine's interpretation of the Apostle, he did not originally aim at showing the wickedness of the Jews. Augustine had used the Pauline statements against the so-called Judaizers, those seeking justification by works of law and boasting of their own righteousness, as a weapon against Pelagius. Luther used the same passages as an instrument against those elements in medieval Roman Catholic theology and church life which questioned or denied the monarchy of grace (Rom. 5:21). In his early (1523) treatise about Jesus the Jew he expressed the hope that now, confronted with the light of the true, the Reformers', interpretation of Jesus Christ's advent and work, the Jews would recognize Jesus as their Messiah. We may smile at this triumphant self-esteem and see in it little progress beyond the attempts to force the conversion of the Jews by means of the crusades or the inquisition. Still, though on his own terms, Luther believed he had become a true lover rather than an opponent of the Jews—precisely in the wake of his enthusiasm for Paul. Things changed sadly, however, during the next twenty years. Disappointed by the lack of enthusiastic Jewish response to the Reformation, Luther wrote in 1543 a second tract on the Jews—a libelous, dirty, mean pamphlet. He not only makes use of the cheapest popular anti-Semitic arguments but dares to give a theological justification to the slander. Thus the *Stürmer* of the Hitler period was enabled to use Luther quotations for his worst witch-hunts. If Zwingli and Calvin did not descend as deeply into the morass of plebeian and ecclesiastical anti-Semitism, they were yet not innocent of continuing occasionally the inherited medieval polemic against the Jews.

We conclude: If not even the Reformers, the rediscoverers of Paul, were led by their discovery of Paul's theology to dismiss, condemn, and fight traditional anti-Semitism—does this not prove that Paul himself was really anti-Semitic? I can only plead for patience and suggest that there may be a considerable difference between Paul and the most ardent Paulinists. It is not fair or necessary to blame the master for the mistakes of his pupils. The same rule applies, as far as I know, to Rabbis too.

6. A certain understanding of Paul's judgment on the Judaizers has influenced, if not prejudiced, the way in which Protestant nineteenth- and twentieth-century Bible scholars have read and explained Jewish writings. Is Paul to be blamed for the prevailing prejudices of Christian theologians in Jewish matters?

Certainly a long way has been trodden—from Justin Martyr's polemic exploitation of his more-or-less correct knowledge of contemporary Judaism, through Nicolas of Lyra's admittedly grateful dependence upon Rashi's research, to John Lightfoot's *Horae Hebraicae*, to the Strack-Billerbeck commentary on the New Testament, to the Schlatter Commentaries, and Gerhard Kittel's *Theological Dictionary of the New Testament*.[1] Christian Bible scholars have sought to delve deeper and deeper into orthodox and heterodox Jewish writings and to create for their Christian readers as fair an image of Judaism between the years 300 B.C. and 300 A.D. as they were able to produce. Outstanding works, like G. F. Moore's *Judaism*,[2] have been highlights on that way; the amount of attention given among Christians to Philo, Josephus, Tannaitic writings, Jewish apocalyptical literature, the newly discovered materials from the caves of the Dead Sea, and early Jewish missionary literature has impressed Jewish scholars. Some of them are willing to admit that research in Judaism done by Christians has made them newly aware of the richness and depth of the Jewish heritage of this period.

But even this great concern shown among Christians for Judaica does not automatically exclude any traits of anti-Semitism. For if the study of Jewish literature is done with the purpose of creating nothing better than a black background against which the light of the New Testament may shine all the brighter, then the Jews are still used as a whipping boy. There are numerous passages in Billerbeck and especially in Kittel in which Jewish teaching is almost monotonously summarized as a lapse from the heights of prophetic teaching. Its heartbeat supposedly lies in promotion of external ceremonies and rituals, in slavery to a legalistic understanding of faith and obedience, and in the proclamation of righteousness by works, i.e., of a meritorious thinking which leads "the Jew" to boast of his election and his good works. No doubt, there are passages in Ezra and Nehemiah, in

Jewish Hellenistic, rabbinical, apocalyptic, and sectarian writings that invite or tolerate such interpretation.

But careful reading of these texts always permits us to discover just as many diametrically opposed utterances that magnify grace alone. Except in very rare cases, Jewish exegesis has never been pursued with the aim of producing one single, unified system of faith or life. In the *Mishna* and the *Talmud* Jewish theologizing is done on a dialectic basis: By combining opposite statements and expositions, it reveals what dialogue is going on when and where people seek to be faithful to the written and oral law. By overplaying one extreme of the pendulum's swing and by underplaying the relevance of the other, Christians have all too often proved less than fair interpreters of *Haggada* and *Halacha*.

Since the Christians' selective concern with such Jewish tendencies that may be dubbed Pelagian was motivated by their interest in an easier, if not better, understanding of Paul, and because it led to a glorification primarily of his (supposedly) anti-Jewish statements, Paul himself had to come under suspicion. For it is he who appears to urge a most intensive and ultimately polemic interpretation of Jewish theology. If the scholarship of so many erudite historians and exegetes should really have proven that Paul was right in his wholesale condemnation of Judaism, how could the conclusion be avoided that Paul himself aimed at destroying the Jewish heritage?

7. Not only Christian scholars but all members of Christian congregations as well as unchurched people who consciously or unconsciously still live from and with scraps of information or evaluation received through the churches' teaching or influence often hurt the Jews without knowing or willing it. He who calls Israel's Bible (the Torah, the Prophets, and the Writings) the "Old Testament"; he who takes pains to prove that Jesus Christ is the "New Law"; he who firmly believes that the Gentile-Christian church is the "new" or the "true people of God"; but also all who believe they are justified in despising circumcision, the celebration of festivals which originated before the birth of Jesus, or the observance of dietary laws—they all hurt

the feelings of Jews. Many Jews have learned in the past two thousand years no longer to protest or bemoan the unnumbered larger or smaller insults and injuries that are continuously showered upon them. Their secret suffering and patience is equaled only by that of the American Negroes whom we white people (even when we are liberals committed to the struggle for civil rights) inadvertently but daily hurt by attitudes, words, and gestures.

Since the life and development of the Gentile Christian churches is unthinkable without Paul's missionary work and the specific message of his preaching, it appears that Paul is to blame for all that has been done to the Jews in the name of Christ. But there was and is also a pre-Christian and a purely secular anti-Semitism. The Pharaoh of the Exodus and (according to the book of Esther) Xerxes of Persia and his advisors were exponents of such an attitude and behavior. Also the Psalms composed during, and in remembrance of, the exile contain evidence of this fact. Before Paul ever reached the Roman capital, the emperor Claudius had pronounced edicts against the Jewish residents of the city, and Hadrian's anti-Jewish legislation hardly had anything to do with Christian influence. Be it admitted that only in very rare cases the life of the dispersed Jews was alleviated after Christianity was tolerated by emperors. Things became worse when Christianity became the state religion. The lot of the Jews was not improved in the time of the medieval power struggles between the popes and the emperors, or later, during the disputes between the church and bourgeois or totalitarian society. Not only notorious enemies of the Jews among educated or uneducated Christians, but many church members who profess religious tolerance or consider themselves friends of Israel have left the Jews to their own fate. They have offended, grieved, or pestered them; they did nothing to prevent their suffering and to stop their defamation.

The sum of the matter presented up till now is unequivocal. Paul is under suspicion of anti-Semitism because many of the best Paulinists have not been free of conceit, contempt, or unconscious or open hostility toward the Jews. We have now to turn to Paul himself and to ask under what conditions he would deserve to be called an anti-Semite and to be treated as such.

B. CRITERIA OF ANTI-SEMITISM

The concept of anti-Semitism with which we have to operate in this part is narrower than the one commonly used. It is impossible to consider Paul the author or an exponent of that sort of anti-Semitism which treats the Jews as an inferior race and discriminates against them as the treacherous, degenerate, greedy, corrupt and corrupting scum of humanity. Except for one passage in a Pauline epistle which will later be quoted extensively (1 Thess. 2:15-16), there are no statements in the Pauline epistles and no records in the book of Acts or other New Testament writings that would justify the assumption that Paul wished the Jews to be treated as a virulent pestilence, that he stood for forced conversion and favored the burning of the temple and of synagogues, or that he wanted the Jews constrained to live in ghettos or even completely extirpated with poisons prepared for insecticide.

But there is another sort of anti-Semitism. I mean a wolf-in-sheep's-clothing type of anti-Semitism which abhors with all decent and enlightened people outright defamation, murder, pogroms, but which resides in the lofty world of religious and philosophical thought, is displayed in books and classrooms, and finds its expression in convictions, sermons, and Sunday school. Even people who are relatively innocent of crude, external, palpable anti-Semitism may be guilty of its more subtle spiritual version. The crude anti-Semitism of the medieval and modern age probably is not of secular origin. Although many attempts have been made to explain it psychologically and to attribute it to man's natural aversion against resident aliens or immigrants, or to his unconscious desire to find a scapegoat for accumulated hostility against any kind of authority or misfortune, its real roots are to be sought elsewhere. Philosophers, poets, and scholars who certainly do not want to spread lies or initiate murder and arson might be accused of having a frightful, if inconspicuous and seldom exposed, responsibility for popular anti-Semitism. While their intention is to divulge pearls of wisdom, they sometimes are found out to have sown dragons' teeth instead.

Is Paul an anti-Semite of this kind? His shield will never be washed clean, if he should be proven the father or defender of one or several of the following doctrines:

1. Israel, after having killed the Messiah it was promised and given by God, and after having refused to believe the message of his resurrection, is no longer the people of God. Rather God's election has now passed away from Israel in order to embrace and glorify the pagan nations. Henceforth, it is the task of the Gentiles who believe in Jesus the Messiah to make the Jews aware of their stiff neck, their hardened heart, and the consequences of their obduracy. Gentile Christians have a right to consider all the historical catastrophes that befall the Jews as so many penalties of God and as a sign of that curse which threatens all apostates from true faith.

2. The law kept holy in Israel from its earliest days to the last breath of martyred rabbis and uncounted faithful Jews was not given by God and Creator, the Lord, the Father, the King and Judge of Israel and the universe, but by another deity or by inferior angelic powers. It is therefore not a real testimony of the full and final will of the gracious God, but a means to increase and reveal man's sin. Ultimately, the law is a curse. But its miserable and dreadful function has been terminated. Since the coming of Jesus Christ the law is replaced by grace, the letter by the Spirit, the works of obedience by faith. Freedom from the law is a prerequisite and a sign of true faith through which alone man is justified. Obedience to God requires no law, no obedience to individual commandments (*mizvoth*), but respect for the Spirit only.

3. Temple and sacrifice, circumcision and other cultic acts, Jewish ethics and customs are not only superfluous but actually opposite to a worship rendered to God in spirit and truth. For all external, statutory, traditional things are inimical to the religion of a free man. Personal experience, innermost emotion, complete passivity, individual decision—in brief, religion of the

heart—wins the victory over formalized and institutionalized cultus. The drama of guilt-feelings and forgiveness, the transition from alienation to acceptance and from unauthentic to authentic existence, even the dramas occurring in the individual man's soul take the place of God's dramatic history with the patriarchs, with Pharaoh, with Israel, with the prophets. Communal life and personal conduct are secondary matters if compared with personal conviction.

4. There are so many elements of truth in Middle Platonism, in Hellenistic Mystery Religions, in Gnostic dualism and Redeemer myths, finally in Stoic morality, that a Christian may gladly learn from them. Not only fragments of the respective thought forms and dictions but decisive elements of the above-mentioned religious trends provide suitable factors for the creation of a new religion, even Christianity. To name a few only, there is the subtle doctrine of mediation between the spiritual and the material world which was offered by Middle Platonism; the experience of sacramental and enthusiastic union with a dying and revived deity which could be taken over from the Mystery Religions; the awareness of the tragic and yet redeemable human existence, sensed by the Gnostics; and finally the noble and practicable ethics of the Stoics, and the not altogether shallow morals of the Hellenistic popular philosophers. A new religion based on such a variety of syncretistic pillars and uniting them in an impressive Pantheon will not fail to appeal to the Gentiles. The renunciation of the authoritarian and rigorous Jewish law will make the new religion all the more acceptable not only for pagans of various nationalities but also for enlightened Jews. After all, such stuff has to be brought to the market that may please the masses because it answers the needs of contemporary man. The success of the Christian mission should warn the Jews who lack the will or the ability to engage in direct missionary action. Where narrow Judaism is bound to fail, syncretistic Christianity triumphantly wins the day. The success of the Christians proves that they are right.

5. There are some reactionary Christians of Jewish descent, who unlike Paul are lacking the gift of logical consistence and

do not discern the spiritual needs of the time. They deserve specific attention and rebuttal. A fitting name for them is "Judaizers." The center of their activity is Jerusalem; their leaders are the Apostles Peter and James, also some unnamed elders and agitators. Their zeal makes them send emissaries to all places at which Paul works. Their theology resembles that of the Gospel of Matthew, the epistle of James, and the letter to the Hebrews. It is the theology of a compromise combining faith in the rule of Christ with continued submission to the rule of the law. It adds works to faith as means of justification. It equates true belief with obedience and shows a slant toward institutional ecclesiology and moralistic or legalistic ethics. It is older than Paul's theology but not superior to it. Since the pagan elements incorporated by Paul into his preaching of Jesus Christ crucified and risen serve the new religion better than does a certain residue of the Jewish religion glorified by the Judaizers, even the most refined way of retaining Jewish motifs in Christian doctrine and practice is to be utterly abhorred and flatly condemned.

The enumeration of criteria for anti-Semitism might be continued. However, the five elements mentioned suffice to establish the evidence that Pauline theology very often gives the impression that this apostle is attacking the Jews in an especially unkind, arrogant, distorting, or hostile manner. Among the selected five arguments, the last might contain the strongest possible proof of Paul's anti-Semitism. That Paul would criticize strongly the teachings which he had received in his youth and that he would react passionately against those Jews who tried to hamper, or use to their own benefit, his missionary enterprise among the Gentiles—this appears psychologically understandable and perhaps forgivable. His argumentation might be taken as a critical response to certain representatives or to some specific features of contemporary Judaism, not as polemics against the essence and substance of the Jewish tradition as such. The fact, however, that Paul turns against some of his Judaeo-Christian brethren only for the reason that they wanted to retain what they were taught from infancy—this seems to furnish the obvious proof that he hated the law as law and that he was hostile to the Jews because they were Jews.

We now have to proceed to the question: Is a doctrine and an attitude of the kind that was outlined in the above five points really present in, and essential to, Paul's teaching? Be it admitted that Pauline interpreters ranging from Augustine through Thomas, Luther, F. C. Baur, to Burton, Bultmann, and Schlier have understood Paul in one or several of the outlined ways. Jewish scholars who took the trouble to seek secondary information on what Paul wanted to say have turned to the Christian commentators on Paul and have found more than a confirmation of their worst suspicions: They read that precisely those things which to them looked most vicious were the very virtues of Paul. I have no quarrel with Jews who assume that nineteen centuries of sometimes scrupulous investigation of Paul should be reliable enough to permit them a judgment on Paul. All too often, though not always, the Christians' image of Paul gave the Jews good reason to consider him an anti-Semite. But I should like to invite my Jewish brethren together with the Christians now to take a further step toward a better understanding of the apostle himself. Among many things not immediately pertinent to the question of his alleged anti-Semitism, recent research in Paul has lead to new aspects, opened up new dimensions, which may eventually force both Christians and Jews to revise and replace worn-out patterns of understanding and assessing this amazing man.

C. SUGGESTIONS FROM NEWER RESEARCH

1. Pauline research has swung from one extreme to another. For decades it was fashionable to collect Gentile-Hellenistic "parallels" to Paul's teachings and to derive from their mere existence the conclusion that Paul was dependent on them. A chapter on Gnostic motifs precedes Bultmann's presentation of Paul's theology.[3] Other writers[4] have concentrated upon the elaboration of Paul's dependence upon Mystery Religions, pagan mysticism, popular philosophy, or other variants of Hellenistic

thought and religion. An opposite movement has been announced in the Schlatter Commentaries and has become strong since the forties of this century: Paul is now explained[5] as a basically Jewish thinker who, despite his work among Gentiles and his use of Greek language and thought forms, can and must be understood in the light of Jewish rabbinical, liturgical, apocalyptical, or sectarian teachings. Opinions vary as to whether a Palestinian-orthodox, a Diaspora-enlightened, or an Apocalyptic-mystical type of Judaism has stamped this man more than other types. Certain is only that Judaism contemporary to Paul existed in so many different layers and followed such divergent strands that the apostle could be thoroughly Jewish even while he followed only one line and lived in tension with certain other forms of Judaism.

It is possible that the pendulum will continue to swing back and forth between these two extremes. But it also is possible that a third alternative of interpreting Paul will gain more and more momentum. If Luther has called the Epistle to the Romans the key to the Old Testament,[6] vice-versa Paul's frequent quotations from the Law, the Prophets, and the Psalms may lead us to regard the Old Testament as the key Paul himself offers to the understanding of his theology. Quotations, allusions, interpretations of biblical concepts and texts are certainly more numerous in Pauline literature than explicit or implicit allusions to pagan, rabbinic, or apocalyptic traditions. Paul did not use the Masoretic canon nor the Masoretic text which received its present shape in early medieval times. But he was familiar with Israel's Holy Scriptures as they were read and explained in the temple, the synagogues, and the schools. He used a Septuagint which differed at places not only from the Hebrew and Aramaic texts but also from the manuscripts underlying the present Septuagint editions.

Recent research in Israel's literature and history, its testimony to God, its faith and traditions (as connected especially with the names of Albrecht Alt, Martin Noth, Gerhard von Rad, and other names associated with their school) but also the investigations of those engaged in the study of biblical words and of the history of religions, have opened a new approach to the treasures of the *Torah*, the *Nebiim*, and the *Ketubim*. It has become evident that Paul's concept of God's saving righteousness is almost identical with the Old Testament meaning of the word *tsedeq-tsedaqa* (translated mostly by "righteousness"), which means a saving act of God.[7] It also has become clear that Paul does not contradict the Exodus tradition, the Book of the Covenant, or Deuteronomy but on the contrary agrees fully with them when he understands and explains the law only on the background of God's covenant and promises granted to Israel. Paul is by no means arbitrary but is following Old Testament precedents when he combines the reference to a specific sacrifice with the emphasis laid upon a special manifestation of grace and love. Finally, Paul's understanding of God's blessing for the Gentiles is thoroughly analogous to the message of Genesis 12:1-3 and of the book of Jonah, not to speak of Deutero-Isaiah. Paul seeks to bring to light the original and historical meaning of the tradition collected in the Mosaic, Prophetic, and Wisdom writings that in different ways is also reflected either in rabbinic, apocalyptic, or heterodox Jewish literature. The claim of Paul to preach nothing but the righteousness of God according to the Law and the Prophets (Rom. 3:21; cf. 1:16-17) looks no longer like wishful thinking on Paul's part. It has become probable that each and every element in Paul's teaching ought to be checked primarily against its roots in the history and canon of Israel and can be explained only in the light of that background.

The Christian Gnostic Marcion presumed to be Paul's disciple when he repudiated large parts of the testimony given in Israel's writings and traditions. That Marcion erred was forcefully asserted by the leading Christian theologians. But though he was declared a heretic, much of his trend of thought has survived. The new studies on Paul call for a complete break with the Marcionite tradition and for a recovery of the Paul of Benjamin whose place is in the heart of the twelve tribes, whether they are in their homeland or in dispersion.

2. The notion that all Pauline statements against justification by works of law and all the correlated utterances against the rule of the law reveal a basic antinomianism has become ripe for

revision. Of course, outright antinomianism—whether it has occurred in sectarian movements splitting off from the Reformation or inside the mainstream of Protestant theology—has always been condemned by Protestant theologians while Catholics have seemed to be safe from the temptation to antinomianism. But when Pauline statements such as ". . . you are not under law but under grace" (Rom. 6:14) or "Christ is the end [*telos*] of the law" (Rom. 10:4) were explained, especially Lutheran theologians showed an inclination to associate the law only with flesh, sin, death or the old aeon and to understand Jesus Christ as the terminator of the law itself. All that was left of the dignity of God's law were functions (*usus*) like the following: First, the law was attributed a certain police function inasmuch as it was permitted to counteract the ground swell of evil and the threatening domination of crime. Second, it served a psychagogic function whenever it led transgressors to realize their sin and prepare them for the salvation found in Christ and in grace alone. Some Lutherans and the Calvinists added a "third use": They considered the law a handrail to help justified and sanctified people live according to God's will. Nineteenth century and later research in the history of religion has added a fourth use, stating that the law represented a (lower) stage in man's development—a level from which he could progress to a higher and more spiritual religion. On the other hand, there had always been Christians who followed the example of Barnabas and Justin Martyr. These men described Jesus Christ as the giver or the embodiment of a "new law." I understand that to Jewish ears most of these doctrines sound antinomian, for they belittle the dignity of God's revelation to Israel, the giving of the law through the hands of Moses, its continued interpretation, and all attempts to keep it day by day.

Now, a closer look at Paul's writings leads to at least three discoveries:

a. Jesus Christ does not mean for Paul the termination or annihilation of the Law; rather he is the purpose and fulfillment of the holy, righteous, and good law of God. The somewhat ambiguous sense of Romans 10:4 (Christ the *telos* of the law)

is interpreted by passages that treat of Christ's obedience to God
and God's law[8] and make it impossible to speak of the abolition
of the law. A Jesus who would have failed to do what (in passages
like Joshua 1, Deuteronomy 17, and by men such as Moses,
Nathan, Jeremiah, and others) is required of the leader or king
of Israel—that he bow to God's law and fulfill it in the interest
of the poor and needy—would never have been called the
"Messiah." According to Paul, Jesus was faithful to the law in
doing what it requires, in accepting the judgment of God which it
contains, in revealing its summary in the commandment of love,
in establishing a kingship and citizenry in which the ruler precedes
his subjects by doing what is right.[9] Because of his obedience,
not because of an act of abolition, Paul calls Jesus Christ the new
Adam (Rom. 5:14, 18-19; Eph. 4:24; 1 Cor. 15:21-22, 45-49).

Paul never understood the law as a curse, a demonic power,
or a world element of idolatrous provenance. Where he seems to
come closest to any affirmation of this kind[10] he was most likely
misunderstood. The phrase "curse of the law" means legitimate
curse, not cursed law; the "law of sin and death" stands in
opposition to God's law (Rom. 7:23); the world elements of
Galatians 4 are not cosmic spirits, stars, or idols, but[11] selected
elements of *human* teaching. According to Paul it is neither God
nor Christ nor the law as such, but sin that makes the law an
opportunity for increasing sin (Rom. 7:7-11). The law in itself
is not "weak and beggarly," but its misinterpretation by the Colossians is a shame (Col. 2:8-9). It is the flesh that "weakens" the
law (Rom. 8:3). The law itself is never called dead or killing,
but its letter read without the aid of the Spirit of the Lord is
dead (Rom. 7:6; 2 Cor. 3:6), and it is man who dies to the law,
once he is legally executed (Gal. 2:19).

Paul summarizes his attitude to the law in the statement,
"Do we then overthrow the law by this faith? By no means! On
the contrary, we uphold the law!" (Rom. 3:31). Why and how?
Because Jesus Christ is for Paul the one man who lives as doer
of the law (Lev. 18:5), the man who by his total obedience
overcomes Adam's disobedience, and takes upon himself God's
judgment and curse. Jesus Christ himself is the righteous one who

lives by faith.[12] The Christians' faith cannot be divorced from the obedience of the Christ. It is his faith, obedience, love that make Christians realize that love is the sum and substance of all the commandments.

b. The opponents of Paul in Galatia were most likely not born Jews but Gentile-Christians. Or else they would not have selected and singled out circumcision from among the other 612 commandments and considered it a substitute for keeping the whole Law.[13] Also if they had been Jewish Christians, they would have *been* circumcised; but Paul says that they were in the process of accepting circumcision.[14] Paul blasts away against ritualistic, pagan-born distorters of the gospel, not against Jews or Jewish Christians.

Paul never scolds unbaptized or baptized Jews for observing among themselves circumcision, dietary laws, a holy calendar. He held nothing against these Jewish laws in themselves; he even observed them himself when he was in Jerusalem or elsewhere among Jews. Galatians 5:6 and 6:15 demonstrate clearly that he did not create a legalism of uncircumcision and set it in opposition to the legalism of circumcision. "For in Christ Jesus neither circumcision nor uncircumcision is of any avail, but faith working through love." "For neither circumcision counts for anything, nor uncircumcision, but a new creation." Some passages,[15] including Paul's utterances regarding the eating of meat offered to idols, prove that under given circumstances he felt free to keep Jewish ceremonial commandments. But he resisted attempts to impose either the whole Jewish Law (all 613 commandments and prohibitions) or selected commandments upon baptized Gentiles. ". . . how can you compel the Gentiles to live like Jews?" (Gal. 2:14). Paul's argumentation somewhat resembles the teaching of those Rabbis who, speaking of the Adamite or Noahite commandments, taught that Gentiles could take part in the coming aeon without having to bear the full load of all commandments.

The Galatian opponents of Paul should not be called "Judaizers." Apart from misleading the reader to take these opponents for Christians of Jewish origin, this name has an anti-Semitic

ring. It suggests that Jewish-born Christians are forcing upon free Gentile Christians some unnecessary or even detrimental elements of their Jewish heritage. Paul never uses a noun that could be rendered by "Judaizers." When, once only, he uses the verb *ioudaizein* ("to live like Jews," Gal. 2:14), this verb designates the action of a Gentile (as in Esther 8:17) who declares himself a Jew: "How can you compel the Gentiles to live like Jews?"

According to Paul the Mosaic Law cannot be imposed upon Gentiles because—as understood in biblical as well as in rabbinic teaching—it is a privilege granted to Israel alone. This law makes sense only upon the basis of God's promise to the Fathers and his covenant with them.[16] Since God did not elect the nations to be his first-born, he also did not give them the Torah. Therefore the Law must not be imposed upon them either by well-meaning or by ill-wishing people. It is common teaching of the Torah, the Prophets, and the Writings that the justification of man in God's judgment depends on God's promise, his covenant, his gracious and saving decree, and not upon some scattered acts of compliance. Therefore, Paul preaches that no flesh (no Jewish flesh either) is justified by law or by works of law. It is his conviction that the Messiah-king, appointed by God, rather than a book or the letter of the Law is the judge and savior of man. The law is a summons to that judgment—for the Jews, not for the Gentiles.[17] Only in 1 Timothy 1:8-10 (a passage probably not written by Paul himself) a universal function of the law is mentioned: ". . . the law is good, if any one uses it lawfully . . ." This passage may have given rise to the speculation about the "uses" of the law. No objection can be made against the contents of the passage, but the anthropological orientation is remarkably different from Paul's theological and historical argumentation about the law in his epistles to the Romans and the Galatians.

H. J. Schoeps[18] argues that Paul's stance on the question of the validity of the law for Gentiles can only be understood by Jews and belongs to an intra-Jewish debate that will never be grasped, let alone arbitrated, by Gentile-born Christians. It is possible that he is right. But it appears more likely that Paul's polemics against

righteousness by works is part of a discussion between Paul and
Gentile Christians. If this be the case, Gentile Christians should
learn to understand what is at stake. Above all, they should then
become aware that they themselves, not some especially malig-
nant Jews or some reactionary Judaeo-Christians, are responsible
for Paul's righteous wrath. There is no evidence available
showing that Paul's *Hebrew* opponents (mentioned in 2 Cor.
11:22) preached that works of law were necessary for salvation.
Passages like Romans 3:31 and 7:12, 14 ("we uphold the law . . .
the law is holy, and the commandment is holy and just and good
. . . We know that the law is spiritual") indicate that Paul did
not intend to abrogate the law. I also doubt that by pointing to
the time limit of the Mosaic Law (in Gal. 3:19-25), he wanted
to interpret *in malam partem* what among Jews was told and
believed to the glorification of the Law.[19] Jewish legends describe
the giving of the law through angels and an intermediary. Paul's
basic intent was certainly not to depreciate the law as such. He
wanted to uphold the glory of the law for Israel and to protect it
from becoming a condition of salvation to be imposed upon
Gentiles who had been confronted with the unified, fulfilled,
personalized will of God—that is, with Jesus the Messiah.

c. It is unlikely that there ever was that basic disagreement
between Jewish and Gentile Christianity which the Tübingen
School of church history writing believed to have discovered and
upon which it thrived. As is convincingly demonstrated by W. D.
Davies,[20] Paul himself was a Judaeo-Christian. Indeed Paul reports
of troubles he had with some false brethren, once also with Peter,
on the question of imposing the law upon Gentiles (Gal. 2:3-5,
11-14). Certainly these false brethren were Jewish-born. But
his own report (Gal. 2:1-10) on an official Jerusalem meeting
about mission work, and Luke's report about another, probably
later, meeting (Acts 15), reveal that the Jerusalem "pillars,"
Peter, James, and John, agreed fully with Paul on all decisive
issues. The Christians in Judaea and Jerusalem had better
things to do with the money Paul had collected for their relief[21]
than to buy tickets for expeditions to follow Paul wherever he
went and to make trouble for him. This is not to deny that in

several places on the mission field troubles arose because of some Jews or Judaeo-Christians[22] who apparently claimed they had been authorized by the Jerusalem congregation. There is, however, no mention that they actually had been commissioned for their agitation. According to Acts 15:24 the Jerusalem leadership and congregation disavowed these anonymous individuals: ". . . some persons from us have troubled you with words, unsettling your minds, although we gave them no instructions." Is this only Luke's way of cluttering history and creating harmony where there was none? There is no indication whatsoever that Paul considered his theology basically different from that of the pillar-apostles and the earliest congregations. In Galatians 2:7-9 the opposite is stated: The same gospel is entrusted by God to Peter and Paul, though for different recipients. The same God works through Peter and Paul. The "pillars" acknowledge gladly the grace given to Paul. And not only the earliest Jerusalem apostles, but "the churches of Christ in Judea . . . glorified God because of me" (Gal. 1:22-24). Of course, since the theology of Jerusalem was never, not even among the earliest Christians living in that city, a closely-knit, unchangeable, systematic unit, Paul could not always be sure of the mother church's attitude toward him. At least once he "submitted" to them the gospel he preached among the Gentiles with fear and trembling "lest somehow I should be running or had run in vain" (Gal. 2:2). But it is obvious that he hoped for unity and that this hope was justified by events. He was given "the right hand of fellowship" (Gal. 2:9).

We proceed now to a third major point where current research challenges the verdict, and maybe also eliminates the suspicion, of Pauline anti-Semitism.

3. Recent research in the history of Israel's prophets has shown that the nineteenth century, especially the idealistic Wellhausian, picture of the biblical prophets was far from accurate. Today it is no longer feasible to oversimplify issues and strain the available data by considering the prophet a man who resists and denounces ceremonies and cultus in the name of social morality; who condemns all institutions in the name of the char-

ismatic individual; who repudiates all external religious acts in the name of personal devotion; who knows of no tradition because he lives from inspiration alone. Much more important things have been brought to light: Prophets have a place and function *within* as well as *against* Israel's institutions. They break with certain customs and criticize current culture by evoking and reviving more ancient traditions. They preach against wicked priests in order to establish true service of God in the temple and on the street. Some of them were priests or came from priestly families. They did not deny or disparage their origin.

For similar reasons it is not possible to see Paul any longer as a rugged individualist who fosters a religion of mystical experience, ethic quietism, psychic introversion, and satanic overestimation of sin—in dead-set opposition to a Jewish or Judaeo-Christian religion of tradition, discipline, corporate responsibility, ethical orientation. Paul did not throw out priestly sacrifice and circumcision. Rather he magnified both by showing what good was done to all mankind by the one sacrifice made on the cross. In Colossians 2:11 (as Ernst Lohmeyer has pointed out in his commentary on this passage) he calls the death of Christ a circumcision (of the race?) with which the Christians were circumcised; and in Ephesians 2:14-16 he reveals that by Christ's sacrificial flesh and blood the wall between Jews and Gentiles was removed. Paul did not abandon all tradition, but rather his writings are spiced with quotes from the Bible; with a method of exegesis learned from the rabbis; with the ability to think in cosmic terms inherited from apocalyptic writers; with elements of Wisdom Literature, which has at all times incorporated non-Jewish elements; with creedal and liturgical formulae taken over from the Judean church and the earliest congregations on Gentile soil. He did not found a religion for the individual existentialist, but rather he founded churches and gave them both a type of doctrine to keep and a staff of respected indigenous presbyters or of his own colleagues. He provided them with detailed and general ethical instructions; he insisted upon common worship, and he knew no faith except the one working in love of the neighbor. As far as we know from the book of Acts, he preached in synagogues until he was thrown out or no longer invited, and he observed the Jewish festivals whenever he could. Not the destruction but the renewal of the Israel of God was his goal. Just as Moses offered his life to God to make, if possible, atonement for his people, so Paul writes, "For I could wish that I myself were accursed and cut off from Christ for the sake of my brethren, my kinsmen by race" (Exod. 32:32, Rom. 9:3).

A man who writes thus is hardly an anti-Semite. Rather he stands in the tradition of the prophets who, as did Jeremiah, had to say in God's name cruel words to his own people. A reformer or prophet is seldom popular among his own. But this does not prove that he hates or despises them. When Paul posits a spiritual temple as over against the building of stone; when he calls for circumcision of the heart, not of the flesh only; when he puts righteousness and love, brotherliness and humility, full obedience and faith above all virtues and accomplishments claimed by some of his contemporaries, then he wages a typically Jewish war. He resists the hardness of heart and the hypocrisy which he perceives. He seeks to move Israel to give honor to God. Israel has been and still is elected to be the living and suffering, the courageous or timid, but always personal evidence and witness of God's existence, covenant, and blessing among the Gentiles. Because he feels called to work for the fulfillment of the Jewish mission among the nations, Paul should never have been quoted for supporting a "mission to the Jews" which treats Jews as if they were a nation like any other nation.

At any rate, precisely Paul's awareness of the responsibility of Israel for the praise of God among the Gentiles makes Paul a true Jew. He was ready to suffer for his calling even from the side of his own people. Jewish history never was, and perhaps never will be, without internal tensions that approximate self-laceration. The Covenanters of Qumran with their stern condemnation of the contemporary official Jewry may serve as just one example. Paul is one among many radicals who has fought with fervor against enemies inside Israel. But the facts that his character was maligned, that he was condemned by many of his own blood, and that many of his followers became anti-Semites prove nothing about himself. Jews have been able to revise their judgment on other unusual saints that have arisen in their midst. Why should it be impossible for them to see that Paul was not an apostate but a true and faithful son of his people? If Christians would cease to make a caricature of him, certainly one precondition for the revision of his defamation among Jews would be met.

4. Paul did not create or possess a system of faith. While there are innumerable attempts to explain his doctrines on Christ, on man, on sin, on atonement, on the church, etc., and to show how they could or should be brought into a systematic whole, the variety of the Pauline epistles and the tension between their contents prevent such enterprises from final success. It is not even sure how many epistles ought to be considered authentic; how many of the canonized Pauline letters were originally a unit; which interpolations, if any, ought to be disregarded; how much Paul identified himself with formulae or whole blocks of materials that he took over from early Christian liturgies and existing tradition. Certainly Paul does not profess a fixed anthropology, soteriology, ecclesiology, eschatology. From occasion to occasion, from letter to letter, if not from chapter to chapter, the images, accents, and actual utterances on similar topics vary. This man was obviously not given at Damascus, or after Damascus in "Arabia," a set of dogmas which he then had to sell or apply in various circumstances to Jews, Gentiles, and Christians alike. After the Damascus revelation he continued to live from further revelations, and these revelations—to judge from all we know about them from the book of Acts—never had the character of dictated, fixed doctrines or of a system of doctrine.[23] Rather this man was given to "learn by doing." He was a practical, missionary theologian rather than a system- or empire-builder. Living as a messenger of Jesus Christ among Gentiles and confronted with ever new situations, he would continually find not only new formulations but new elements, dimensions, insights to put before his listeners and readers. Like anybody else, the longer he lived, the more he was able to learn.

In this process he sought imperturbably to serve Jesus Christ alone (Gal. 1:10). His master made him free not to become stuck in positions taken earlier, but to move forward. He did not always speak of "justification." While he always preached Christ crucified and risen,[24] he placed more emphasis on his death in one context, and more on his resurrection or second advent in another. Sometimes he speaks of the first and the second Adam, sometimes of the old and the new man. At times the Old Testament argument is essential to his writing, but at other times there are almost no quotes or implicit references. In some letters the *parousia* of Jesus Christ is expected within a brief time; in others it seems not to be preeminent. Paul was not a machine grinding out doctrines, nor did he work like a computer, producing a dogma by the combination of certain given facts, rules, or methods. He was a living man who sought to be a faithful witness to God in the midst of different, changing, and often adverse circumstances.

Both the stability and the changeability of Paul can be observed specifically in his doctrinary statements on those Jews who have not been baptized:

1 Thessalonians 2:15-16[25] is a dreadful text—explicable only upon the background of a very acute persecution in which probably worse things happened than the harassments recorded in Acts 17:5-13.[26] Paul wrote to the Thessalonians, "[The Jews] killed both the Lord Jesus and the prophets, and drove us out, and displease God and oppose all men by hindering us from speaking to the Gentiles that they may be saved—so as always to fill up the measure of their sins. But God's wrath has come upon them at last!" Not only are these verses prone to misuse by people who are anti-Semites by disposition or education, but they are in themselves passionate, generalizing, hateful. Paul appears to refer to the death of Jesus, Jewish ill will against the Gentiles, the wrath of God, in order to justify what anyway has been in his heart and upon his lips. These verses may indeed be called a sample of that anti-Semitism which sometimes is found not only among Gentiles but in worse form among desperate Jews. The quote appears plain and powerful enough to negate *all* we have said so far!

But more statements of Paul have to be considered. In Galatians 4:21-31 Paul alludes to the story of the slave girl Hagar and her son Ishmael, who according to Sarah's wish and God's command were "cast out" into the wilderness by Abraham and thereby deprived of any inheritance in Abraham's patrimony. In this typological-allegorical interpretation Paul equates Sinai, Hagar, and her offspring with the "present Jerusalem" where thralldom is the order of the day. Freedom is only where the covenant represented by Sarah, Isaac, and his descendants is valid. The Spirit-born Isaac is treated as the prototype of Christ and the Christians; the slave child Ishmael, as corresponding to the Jews. The application seems clear: The Jews who do not believe in Jesus the Messiah are thrown out from God's house. They have no part of God's blessing; theirs is the lot of most miserable slaves and wandering nomads. In this context Paul fails to mention that according to the Genesis story (Gen. 16 and 21) God also protected and multiplied Ishmael.

When we follow the sequence of Paul's writings which has, with a fair amount of probability, been established by historical scholars of the last decades, a passage in 1 Corinthians (2:8) is to be mentioned next. Here the crucifixion of Jesus Christ is ascribed to "the rulers of this age." The identity of these rulers is not defined; Paul most likely thought of demonic powers which were at work behind the scenes of the Jerusalem of the year 30 and operated through and in both the Jewish and the Roman authorities. Their decision and deed Paul ascribed to ignorance: "None of the rulers of this age understood this; for if they had, they would not have crucified the Lord of glory." Cf. Acts 13:27, "For those who live in Jerusalem and their rulers . . . did not recognize him [the Messiah Jesus]." Here[27] ignorance appears to be mentioned as a mitigating circumstance. Deliberate malice is not imputed to the Jews, and there is no hint saying that the contemporary Jewish authorities, much less all earlier and later Jews, were willful "deicides." Jews who take offense at the crucified Jesus are in Paul's opinion not worse than Gentiles for whom the crucified Christ is "folly" (1 Cor. 1:23).

In 2 Corinthians 3:4-18 the indictment or condemnation of the Jews is again attenuated. A veil, comparable to the one worn by Moses to hide the splendor of God reflected on his face, is said to lie over the hearts of the Jews. Thus when they read the Scriptures, they cannot perceive the glory of the Lord which is seen when the Scriptures are read with unveiled face. It is not said that Israel is partially or wholly rejected by God. But Israel is described as blindfolded. While the designation of Moses' ministry as a "ministry of death" and of "damnation" has a polemic ring, the glory of the legislation on Mount Sinai is yet not denied. Only because of the greater and permanent splendor of the new covenant made through Jesus Christ, is the splendor of the former dispensation boldly pronounced to have faded away, surpassed by the glory which comes through Christ from the Lord who is the Spirit.

In 2 Corinthians 3 and Galatians 4, the references to the new covenant and to the covenant with the "free" are not based upon something completely foreign to Israel's history and Scriptures. Rather Paul attempts to show in both passages that throughout God's history with Israel a difference is made between covenant and covenant, or between people and people. Thus, in agreement with an early Christian tradition, Paul alludes (in 1 Cor. 11:25) to the new covenant promised already by the prophet Jeremiah. The book of Genesis itself differentiates sharply between Sarah and Hagar and between each one's offspring. God's promise alone decides who is the true son (cf. Rom. 9:7-9). Only because of his election to a specific ministry Moses may stand before the Lord with unveiled face and has to cover his face when he appears before the people—this is asserted already by the Sinai tradition, not by Paul only. Paul does not invent the notion that throughout Israel's history God is a God who freely elects. The apostle finds prototypes of both Jews and Christians in the very books of the Law. Israel's Bible itself keeps Jews and Christians together. Paul does not intend to be wiser than the book he quotes from. While he recognizes that his own and the church's ministry is analogous to specific features of the history of God and man recorded in the Bible, he does not deny that other men and events also belong to that history. He participates in the dialogue, the dialectics, and the tension that form the total of Israel's history.

Different again is the well-known simile of the olive tree and its branches, by which Paul in Romans 11:16-24 illustrates the relationship between the church and Israel. There is the holy root (and stem)—Israel. There are branches that were cut off and wild branches that were grafted in their place—meaning some Jews and those among the Gentiles who believe in Jesus Christ. It looks as if Paul wanted to say just one thing: Israel has forfeited its privilege and is "out"; the Gentiles were graciously elected and are now "in." But the first impression is erroneous. What Paul drives at is to remind the Gentiles of their insertion into the holy root, Israel. He makes them aware of their adoption by sheer grace, warns them against boasting of their new position upon the sacred root. He goes as far as to tell them that God—unlike a horticulturist!—is able and willing to reengraft the original shoots into the original olive tree. Precisely the opposite to the popular self-understanding of some Christians is found here. Far from saying that the Gentile Christians are now God's people at the expense of Jews, Paul shows that to be God's people means to participate in the history of God with Israel. As already mentioned above, Paul neither knows nor uses the concepts of a "new" or "true people of God." Nobody can be a member of God's people without belonging to Israel and sharing the ups and downs of God's history with his elect. Only those are truly members of his people who submit to God's election of the rejected and to his faithfulness toward the unfaithful. They accept the suffering of God's servant, the representative ministry of one for the benefit and salvation of many. God does not reject eternally; he remains true to his way of election, which from the beginning has been known as his faithfulness to, and his justification of, undeserving man.

The climax of Paul's teaching on Israel is found in Ephesians. Because of linguistic, historical, and doctrinal reasons many Bible scholars are unable to accept Paul as its author. They still have to admit that the contents of Ephesians show strong influences of Pauline thought. Perhaps the epistle is Pauline just because of its astonishing deviations from other, unquestionably Pauline, statements. For only Paul himself, but scarcely a Paulinist, could afford to move ahead in his thinking as radically as this epistle shows. At any rate, even if Ephesians should not have been written by Paul himself, this epistle is a marvelous example of the unfolding and maturing of Pauline thought and teaching.

According to Ephesians 2:11-22 the effect of Christ's sacrificial death lies in the acceptance of Gentiles into the citizenry of God's people. Those who once were far off, strangers to the commonwealth of Israel, have been brought near to the covenant of promise. Through Christ's death on the cross, Jews and Gentiles who formerly had been hostile to each other have been made one. In Christ the two have been created anew and are now "one new man." This new man is not identical with each individual Judaeo- or Gentile-Christian who believes in Jesus Christ. He rather comprises at least two individuals, one of Jewish and the other of Gentile descent, who together approach God the Father in common worship.

While this worship is publicly apparent wherever the church acknowledges Jesus Christ's work and praises God in words, hymns, deeds, and sufferings, the author does not limit Christ's work to the faithful only. In this passage those who are circumcised—regardless of whether they believe in Jesus Christ or not—are called God's people and saints. The Gentiles are not saved by forming a new or true people, but they are added to "the household of God." It is not assumed that only part of Israel are citizens in God's kingdom. What is emphasized is the novelty that now Gentiles are made fellow citizens and heirs and are given equal rights with those who always had been God's own people and partakers of "God's life" (cf. Eph. 2:6, 3:6, 4:18). Though not all Jews confess Jesus as the Messiah, Israel's special function is not over with the Messiah's coming. According to Ephesians 2:1-10 and its context, it is the special function of Israel to remind the Gentile-born Christians that by sheer grace alone they are called out of spiritual death to new life and are associated to the house of promise and hope.

What then is the role of faith? It reveals and bears witness to the unity of the Gentiles who had been dead in sins with the Jews, who also were saved from God's wrath. This unity is con-

fessed where there is "one faith, one baptism."[28] Faith and confession are part of Christ's work, just as the ending of the hostility, the making of peace, the creation of the new man are
brought about not by man's belief, but by Jesus Christ's death. In
faith this is acknowledged, celebrated, proclaimed. Peace between
Israel and the nations and peace between God and man is the
content or subject matter of faith, not a product of individual
conversion or belief. This may be why in Ephesians 2:11-22
Christ's work is described at length without a single reference to
faith.

Therefore it cannot be claimed that the Jews are God's people only under the condition that they believe in Jesus the Messiah. Faith, according to Ephesians, ultimately designates the
faith of Jesus Christ himself to which all men are invited (Eph.
4:13, 3:12). Even at the present time it manifests itself as a living
and efficient power. Faith of both Jews and Christians consists of
a solid stance upon a ground laid *before* the conversion of any
individual Jew or Gentile. This ground is provided by Jesus
Christ's uniting work, even by his death on the cross which took
place "while we were yet helpless . . . yet sinners . . . enemies [of
God]" (Rom. 5:6-10).

Looking back upon the way on which we followed Paul's
thought from 1 Thessalonians to Ephesians, we observe a drastic
change not only of language and imagery but also of content.
There is certainly not a watertight system of thought before us
and specifically not one hard-boiled opinion or judgment on "the
Jews." But what starts with extremely unfriendly utterances in 1
Thessalonians ends up in the praise of peace and unity found in
Ephesians. And on the road from one to the other there are sta-
tions having open windows toward the beginning and the end of
the way. Some of Paul's early statements are subject to an anti-
Semitic interpretation, but they are open also for deeper and
friendlier reflection. True to its trend and message, Ephesians
has left behind and treated as overcome all signs of bitterness and
hostility. In case Paul himself was not—in the last years of his
life—the author of Ephesians, it would have to be assumed that
he never reached the end of the way we followed; it is still indu-

bitable that he wrote Romans and that Romans 11 comes close to Ephesians 2. What if not Paul himself but one of his pupils added the crown to his work? Nothing is detracted from Paul's relevance if he had a follower who was able to go further than his master! Certain is that the early church's inclusion of Ephesians in the Pauline corpus and in the New Testament canon amounts to urgent advice for the worldwide church of all centuries to move onward with Paul on the way he was following.

Obedience to the Bible is less than perfect when it relies exclusively on certain isolated biblical passages. Literal understanding and legalistic obsequiousness to singled-out verses do not prove a man obedient and faithful to God. God gave Israel the Torah as a "directive" or signpost so that his people might move ahead on a specific way and at the same time recognize God's way of coming to his elect. Equally, the theology of Paul consists of signposts placed under different circumstances at different places. To learn from Paul, as from any biblical author, means to trust his directives and to move ahead accordingly. If anyone should refuse to abandon a once-taken position for the sake of a more adequate understanding of God's way, certain utterances of Paul might prove for him as deadly as any one singled-out phrase of any other script. Pauline theology is not a system composed of infallible proclamations. It rather has to be understood as a guide leading to the worship and service of the Lord.

5. There is one element in Paul's teaching which defies by nature inclusion in a system. I mean his reference to the future appearance of Jesus Christ in his glory, the *parousia*.[29] Since Albert Schweitzer,[30] Pauline scholars have no longer been able to disregard the presence of a strong apocalyptic element in Paul. Careful British scholars like W. D. Davies and C. K. Barrett, the Tübingen professor Ernst Käsemann,[31] and the Jewish historian of religion H. J. Schoeps have put equal emphasis on this element —though for different reasons and with different results.

The relation of Paul's apocalyptical preaching to Jewish orthodox theology is twofold. Inasmuch as Paul's word "now" has an eschatological ring,[32] it asserts what Jews deny: With Jesus Christ "the end of the ages has come" and the "new creation" is already at hand.[33] Nevertheless the clash between Paul and the Jews need not lead to mutual excommunication. As was stated before, many Jewish teachers, among them Rabbi Aqiba, have believed, as did Paul, in the fulfillment of an eschatological promise and have identified it with a Messianic figure of their time. Though the identification of a certain person with the hoped-for Messiah often caused great sufferings to Israel, yet these teachers were not ranked with pagan anti-Semites. The large majority of the Jews may not agree with Paul's preaching of the advent, the passion and resurrection of Jesus the Messiah. They observe too little, if any, change in world history that would prove him to be the true Messiah. Their disagreement with Paul at this specific point, however, does not force them to deny the Jewish character of his theology or to consider him an enemy of all things Jewish.

A second, this time a positive, relationship of Paul to Jewish expectation needs to be pointed out. Paul himself is convinced that Jesus has been bodily raised and that it was the crucified Jesus who appeared alive before his eyes on the Damascus road as he had appeared earlier to many of the earliest disciples. But though Paul took the trouble to collate all available traditions of the names and numbers of eyewitnesses (1 Cor. 15:5-8), he yet knew that he could not show or prove the resurrected one to any Jew or Gentile in Palestine, Asia, Greece, or Rome. The message of the crucified and risen Jesus Christ contained many references to events in history. But it did not rely on historical proof. Rather it called for faith. If you "believe in your heart that God raised him from the dead, you will be saved" (Rom. 10:9); ". . . and so you believed" (1 Cor. 15:11). The existence of congregations praising God because of the witness given by Christ's apostle may come close to a proof of the authenticity of his apostolate;[34] it is still not yet a proof of Jesus' Messiahship. Worldwide evidence of Jesus Christ's identity and of the success and validity of his work will be given only when he appears in glory, as judge of the living and the dead, to be honored by all powers in heaven, on earth, and under the earth (cf. Phil. 2:9-11).

In the expectation and in descriptions of that day of revelation and judgment,[35] Paul speaks without inhibition of good works, of reward, of a harvest, of a verdict according to works. Since he had at other places passionately repudiated the value of works for justification, it was long believed that the real Paul, the Christian Paul, was to be found only where he engaged in polemics against works, whereas another Paul, a man still bound by Jewish notions, was speaking of a judgment according to works. To the same extent as the difference between Paul and the Judaizers was acclaimed, his all-too-obvious agreement with Jewish expectations was regretted. Fortunately there have appeared three recent books on Paul[36] whose authors insist on pointing out that justification "without works of law" and "judgment according to works" must not be understood as contradictory terms. If the combination of both still remains a puzzling enterprise and will continue to create difficulties for Paul's interpreters, careful expositors have yet no right to solve the problem by sweeping one essential part of Paul's doctrine under the rug. It is false to assume that Paul's utterances on the last judgment are irrelevant for Christians. Their close relationship to Jewish expectations proves the ultimate identity of Jewish and Christian hope rather than a flaw in Paul's thought and preaching.

Paul's theology is a theology of hope. His faith is based upon the hope for the public appearance of the Messiah on earth and hope for the change that will be brought about through him. Paul expects the triumph of God, of grace, of life, of righteousness, of peace. He is convinced that God's triumph will not crush but glorify man. In living from and for this hope, Paul neither refused nor combated the hope for resurrection which is vital to Jewish prayer, teaching, and ethics. On the contrary, he expressed it with vigor and he was ready to die for it. Luke reports that Paul himself, on at least one occasion (Acts 23:6), professed his relation to Israel with the following words: "Brethren, I am a Pharisee, a son of Pharisees; with respect to the hope and the resurrection of the dead I am on trial."

III

ISRAEL AND THE CHURCH
IN PAUL'S EPISTLE TO THE EPHESIANS

———————

A. EPHESIANS AMONG THE PAULINE EPISTLES

Ernst Percy's study in the linguistic, thematic, and theological characteristics of Ephesians[1] shows how dispensable are the fanciful theories about the origin and how superfluous is the exasperating search for a post-apostolic author of this epistle. Percy's arguments for Pauline authorship appear convincing. The somewhat troubling peculiarities of language and content which distinguish this epistle from the so-called authentic epistles of Paul are also found in those Pauline passages where the Apostle interrupts his dogmatical or ethical teaching with a prayer or a hymn-like exclamation.[2] Although the style, structure, and substance of Ephesians may present some traits which contrast with other works of the Apostle, their prayerlike or liturgical character does not warrant the quest for an unknown author. Much less does it entitle the reader to attribute this letter to a deutero-Paulinist who failed to fully understand his master. Although the exact date and address of this letter still are a matter of conjecture, its message clearly speaks for Pauline authorship.[3]

This proposition, however, should not be defended by a list of the similarities of Ephesians with the rest of the Pauline corpus. More strongly than all analogies, the distinctions and peculiarities of this epistle point to Paul as its author. A disciple or imitator of the Apostle would probably have kept closely to his master's teaching. He would have avoided going beyond what his master had said. Only the master himself was free not to feel bound by earlier utterances or restricted by a party platform. An *epigone* would have wished to give the impression of being a true Paulinist. But Paul himself was no Paulinist.

Ephesians says amazing things about the broken wall (2:14) and the peace made and preached by Christ to those far and near (2:13-17); about the revelation of the mystery (3:1 ff.) and the gift of the apostolate and the other ministries of the word (3:1 ff., 4:7-13); about the church as a citizenry and as a growing temple of God, or as the body and bride of Christ;[4] about the knowledge given to the church in order to be passed on to the principalities and powers.[5] Most of the elements which are typical of Ephesians are also contained in the epistles to the Romans, the Galatians, the Corinthians, the Philippians. But in Ephesians lines are extended and emphatic accents set where other Pauline letters give no more than feeble hints.

To the elements uniquely emphasized in Ephesians belongs its doctrine on the church. Ephesians speaks more—and more clearly—than the rest of the Pauline epistles about the one, holy, apostolic, and catholic church. It counteracts any wildly congregationalist interpretation or exploitation, for example, of the epistles to the Corinthians. What is said in this epistle about the origin, essence, unity, purpose of the church can certainly be stated, but never simply explained, in the categories and with the criteria of psychology and sociology. The coming and work of the Messiah Jesus—the so-called Christology—determine the church's life and function. In vain a reader of Ephesians will search for, or attempt to construct, an ontology and teleology of the church that might even in the slightest degree be independent of the eternal place and the past, present, and future work of Christ. Neither in a neo-Platonist nor a Gnostic, neither in an idealistic nor a materialistic sense is the church considered to be an emanation or extension (of the divinity or humanity) of Jesus Christ. Nor is it built upon the experiences of individuals or upon the laws of community and group dynamics. Rather everything said about the church's essence and existence has a functional and operative character. According to this epistle the church exists because in his eternal plan ("in Christ") God wanted and chose it (1:4 ff.). In the fulness of time, through the coming and work of Jesus Christ, God executed and proclaimed this plan (1:10; 2:13 ff.). Again "in Christ," God gave the church a knowledge that will increase and a witness that is to be borne in the world.[6] The church is not a divine or impersonal entity that has to expand over the world and finally absorb it. Rather she is the personal God's chosen, created, sustained personal bride (5:24-32). She is his witness for all the world and all future ages (2:7, 3:10). She is the established evidence of how great and how costly is God's love and what response of man is pleasing to him.

The constitution of the church is, according to this epistle, a dynamic affair. It serves nothing else but the praise of God.[7] What is said about God's elect, the citizenry, the house, the body, the bride, is altogether a hymn of adoration praising the living God for the wondrous creation of a new man. No definition could or should take the place of this magnificat. What we learn in Ephesians about the spirit, the knowledge, the word, the service, and the mission cannot be separated from the worship of God. The elaboration of an invariable, static church constitution and a once-for-all fixed order of worship would contradict the very purpose of this epistle and go beyond its thought. The love relationship of Christians to one another and their missionary responsibility toward the world call for ever new, free ethical decisions. It is impossible for these stimuli to complete and spontaneous response to God to be pressed into a rigid system or a moral casuistry.

The constitution and order of the church is identical with her living and specific relationship to God and to the world. The ecclesiology of Ephesians can be summed up by the key word "love."[8] As does the double commandment of love in the Synoptic Gospels (Matt. 22:34-40), so Ephesians points to the source, the driving force, and the goal of the life of God's elect. God's gift to his beloved is love of God and of one's fellowman (cf. Rom. 5:5).

This foundation of the church is qualified and specified in a surprising way. As little as anywhere else in the New Testament does the author speak of God and man in general. Christ, his cross and his resurrection, the Spirit and his work qualify everything. But this is not all! The "life of God" of which Paul speaks (4:18) is manifest already in the history of Israel (2:12). The new man, created by God after his likeness, who is to be "put on" (4:24; cf. Col. 3:10) is created from the Jews and Gentiles (2:15). The free access now opened to God (3:12; cf. Rom. 5:2) is an access of "both," i.e., of Jews and Gentiles (Eph. 2:18). An interpreter of Ephesians can speak neither of God's acts for mankind nor of man's stand before God without at the same time speaking of Israel. The question must therefore be asked: Should the Christians' relationship and behavior toward Israel be the criterion of their faith in the living God and of their love?

Among the Pauline epistles addressed to a congregation, Ephesians is the only one which explicitly is written to Gentile-Christian church members alone.[9] The recipients of this letter are obviously linked to Israel (in Christ) "before the foundation of the world" (1:4-14), by the cross (through Christ's atoning sacrifice, 2:13-16), and by God's continued demonstration of mercy and grace (through faith, 2:1-9). They are in danger of falling back into their former pagan ways (4:17-19). They are reminded that they belong together with Israel, not only because both "were by nature children of wrath" (2:3), but much more since they have become "fellow citizens with the saints and members of the household of God" (2:19), "fellow heirs" (3:6), and parts of one and the same growing body (4:15 f.) through "the bond of peace" (4:3).

The emphatic repetition of the theme of Jewish-Gentile unity comes as a surprise. It is anticipated in Galatians (2:11-21, 3:26-29) and Romans (1-3, 9-11). The epistle to the Romans does contain passages addressed exclusively to Jewish-born and Gentile-born Christians respectively (2:17-29, 11:13-24), but as a whole it is not directed toward only one group in the church. The same is true of Galatians and Philippians. Why, then, is Ephesians destined for Gentile-Christians only? Acts 18:19 ff. leaves no doubt that quite a few unbaptized and baptized Jews lived in and around Ephesus. It will not do to disparage the seeming contradiction between Acts and Ephesians by stating that Ephesians was not directed to the church in Ephesus. There are good rea-

sons—solid evidence in the better Greek manuscripts—for questioning the authenticity of this epistle's address. But even if the
letter went to a wide circle of probably newly-baptized Christians
who did not know Paul personally, two amazing facts remain:
Only Christians of Gentile origin are here addressed. And they
are told that without a most intimate connection with Israel they
cannot be Christians. The baptized Gentiles are, according to
this epistle, not the legal successors of God's chosen people,
Israel. Only together with Israel are they worshippers of one
Father, citizens of God's Kingdom, members of God's household
(2:18-19). No one can call himself a Christian and forget that he
shares in the privilege that first has been accorded to Israel alone.
There is only *one* Christian church: the church from Israel and
from the Gentiles.

Since the predominantly Gentile-Christian church of today
finds herself in a situation similar to the one Paul presupposed
in Ephesus, and since she is characterized by much of the same
forgetfulness and conceit as was present in the church in Ephesus, this epistle calls for special attention. A biblical parable can
facilitate the understanding of Ephesians.

The Gentiles' adoption into the household of God is comparable to the prodigal son's reception in his father's house. The
prodigal finds in the father's house not only the father and his
servants, but also his brother who has never left home but by
the sweat of his brow has worked on his father's estate (Luke 15:
11-32).

We cannot prove and we do not want to assert that there is a
literary connection between this parable and the epistle to the
Ephesians. Nevertheless this story may serve to clarify and to
illustrate what Ephesians has to say about the relationship between Jews and Gentiles. Moreover it is not altogether out of
question that by this parable Luke meant to portray more than
only the relationship between sinful and righteous men inside
Israel. In anticipation of what he was to describe in the Acts of
the Apostles, he also aimed at describing the relationship between Gentiles and Jews. In Ephesians some elements of the
parable are recurring: the contrast between previous deadness

and present life through resuscitation; between estrangement and homecoming or access to the father; between loss of all rights and installation or sealing by the father into the rights of son and heir; between shameful living and undeserved glorification. Here and there the hostility between one man who is always near and another who was distant plays a great but not a final role. The love of the father is greater than the power of enmity.

There is, however, at least one decisive difference of content and intention between the gospel story and Ephesians. Whereas the Lucan parable ends with the father's appeal to him who always was at home, Ephesians is addressed to those who were alienated, strangers, hopeless, foolish, delivered to licentiousness (Eph. 2:12, 4:17-19). If we follow Ephesians, it is not so much the attitude of the older brother to the younger as the relationship of the younger to the older which is now decisive. Paul makes it very clear that the very life, prayer, and witness of the church are at stake when this relationship is denied or disturbed.

According to Ephesians it would be wrong, unrealistic, fateful, if not suicidal for the church, if her Gentile-Christian members segregated themselves from their Jewish brethren and regarded themselves as superior. The church is in no position to boast. Rather she is in danger of losing her right of existence unless she remembers that this right was granted her by that God who always was and is the God of Israel. It would prove disastrous for the church if ever she were to forget the sequence of God's acts in history and thus declare herself the sole possessor or trustee of truth and salvation.

Vainglorious pretentions and blindfolded triumphalism are found mostly in churches whose majority is of pagan origin. They are voiced where the Christendom of Gentile Christians was made the criterion of Christianity and where the church did not "remember" God's dispensation and the strategy of his plan.

A series of Pauline texts may be quoted for justifying a certain pharisaical attitude of the Christians toward the Jews.[10] In many texts the church appears to be clearly set apart from and opposite to Israel. Mention is made of "the Jews," the new covenant, the Israel of God. But because these texts are sometimes used for supporting deep-rooted prejudices against Israel and all Jews, the epistle to the Ephesians should also be heard. Ephesians may force the reader of all Pauline epistles to search for a more careful interpretation and a more conscientious application of the above-mentioned passages.

B. INTERPRETATION OF KEY TEXTS

The passages which are of particular relevance to our subject are the following:[11]

Ephesians 1:11-14: "In Christ *we* have been destined before and appointed . . . to be (or, to live) for a praise of his glory—we who were the first to set our hope upon Christ. In him *you* also . . . were sealed by the promised Holy Spirit . . . to the praise of his glory."

We note that in these verses two parallel statements are made: "We have been destined . . . for a praise of his glory"; "you . . . were sealed . . . to the praise of his glory." The explicit distinction between "we" and "you" is hardly rhetorical. As is the case in other epistles of Paul, "we" might mean Paul (sometimes together with his colleagues) and "you," the addressees. The priority of those who were the first to hope over those who "at that time . . . had no hope" (2:11-12) might consist in the precedence of Paul's conversion over that of the Ephesians, of the special function fulfilled by the Apostle among the congregations, or of his and other Judaeo-Christians' Jewish descent. In no case does this priority imply a qualitative superiority. For in Ephesians 2:1-5 it is made clear that no difference in quality or in position before God is meant: "you were dead through the trespasses and sins in which you walked . . . Among these we all once lived . . . we were by nature children of wrath, like the rest of mankind. But God . . . when we were dead through our trespasses, made us [and you] alive together . . ." (R.S.V.). As to sin and salvation by grace there is obviously "no distinction" (cf. Rom. 3:22) between Paul and all other Christians, between those converted earlier or later, or between all Judaeo- and Gentile Christians.

Why, then, does he make a distinction at all between "we" and "you"? The dignity of the apostolic ministry is discussed not in Ephesians 1:3-14, but in 3:1 ff.[12] Ephesians 2:11-12 shows clearly that the differentiation is made in order to point out a historic sequence of two groups of men. It is the Gentiles who were yet without hope, while others already ("first," 1:12, R.S.V.) had a firm hope. Opposite the hopeless Gentiles stands, according to 2:11-12, the commonwealth of Israel. Those "hoping first" must therefore be the Jews who were God's "holy ones," his "citizens," "members of God's household" before Gentiles were joined to them (2:19). Paul reminds the Gentile-born Christians of the foundation upon which they are grounded, i.e., the history of the "covenants of promise" (2:12, R.S.V.) which at first seemed to comprehend Israel alone. Before the coming of Christ it was not disclosed that the covenants and the promise included the Gentiles (3:5-6).

The following two passages will show the meaning of the historical differentiation between the "we" and the "you."

Ephesians 2:11-20: "Remember that you were once Gentiles in the flesh, called the uncircumcision by those who call themselves the circumcision (that operation) which was made by hand in the flesh. Remember that at that time you were without the Messiah, alienated from the commonwealth of Israel and strangers to the covenants of promise, having no hope, and godless in the world. But now in Jesus the Messiah you who once were far have become near through the blood of the Messiah. For he is our peace; he made the two (things? parties? groups? men? peoples?) one. In his flesh, he destroyed the intermediate wall, the enmity. He abrogated the law of ordinances in statutes in order to create in him out of the two (men, or peoples) one new man by making peace, and in order to reconcile them both in one body to God by killing in himself the enmity. He came and preached peace to you who are far, and peace to those near. For through him we both have access to the Father in one Spirit. Therefore you are no more strangers and sojourners, but you are fellow citizens of the saints and members of God's household, built upon the foundation of the apostles and prophets, the Mes-

siah Jesus himself being the capstone . . . a structure joined together . . . you are being built together . . ."

Circumcision, membership in a household and citizenship,
promise, covenants, being near—all these features characterize
Israel. Uncircumcision, existence as strangers and sojourners,
hopelessness, godlessness, being far off—these are the corresponding characteristics of the Gentiles. The difference between
the two is objectively marked by an intermediate wall, subjec-
tively by hostility. The separation is not just a coincidence but
was established by detailed casuistic statutes of law. The law, in
turn, was originally a sign of God's election. May the Gentile-
Christian Ephesians remember on which side of the wall they
once stood (2:11-12); may they desist from the morals of the outside (4:17-19). Hostility not only between man and man but also
between man and God used to be the order of the former days, as
long as the wall of separation was standing. But by God's inter-
vention, separation and war were ended, peace was made, and
communion was established. In this passage Paul describes the
work of Jesus Christ in magnificent one-sidedness. It consists of
the abrogation of hostility. Its essence is the creation and building of a new man, a man who without fear may come and live
and grow in the presence of God. May the Ephesians remember
the fact and the mode by which they began to live as one new
man!

But what is meant by the "one new man" in 2:15? He
is hardly identical with Jesus Christ, the new or last Adam;
otherwise, this verse could not go on saying that Christ created
him in himself. He may have been created out of him, like Eve of
Adam. But Christ did not create himself. Should a Christian personality be meant, or a total of such personalities, i.e., a Christian
collective consisting of uniform individuals? Such a personality
might supersede all differences between sexes, generations, social
positions. Then man ought to treat fellowman, one congregation
ought to treat a fellow congregation, the church ought to treat
the world, as equals and seek to establish and demonstrate the
concept of a uniform humanity at the expense of all individual-
ity. Is it the idea or ideal of a Christian that Paul has in mind

when he speaks of the one new man, created by God (4:24), or created by Christ in Christ (2:15)? Has Paul a model or pattern in mind when in Galatians 3:28[13] he says that all are "one in Christ" and that there is "neither Jew nor Greek . . . slave nor free . . . male nor female"? Certainly some relevant passages are often understood this way. The difference of Jews and Gentiles, but with it also the differences between male and female, older and younger, etc., are then denied or suppressed. The Christian church becomes the place for forcing all men into a stereotype. If it is a *Christian* uniform, it is still a uniform that is considered the solution of all problems of strife or diversity. The legitimacy of such leveling performed in the name of the individual or collective "Christian personality," is, however, questionable. For Paul, the new man is obviously not an ahistorical, sexless, international and intercultural, transsocial and transeconomical superman!

The one new man, rather than a number of separately renewed individuals, is kept together by the bond of peace (Eph. 4:3). No reference is made to uniformity, except to conformity with Christ (Rom. 8:29). Within the newness and unity brought by Christ, Paul recognizes distinctions of origin, age, sex; and he is far from seeking their extinction. Jews and Gentiles, men and women, parents and children, free-men and slaves, receive different and specific admonitions in Galatians and Romans, and especially in the *Haustafeln*.[14] Each one of them is deemed worthy of special exhortation. The ground of such exhortation is not a harking back upon sad conditions prevailing in and surviving from the first creation, but the proclaimed unison which is the content and result of the new creation of man. The one new man consists of several men who are joined together. Consequently, there is only one new man, not several new men or a collective of new personalities—if Paul's message of Ephesians 2:15 is taken at all seriously in its context. The Pauline *kerygma* attests as strongly as Pauline ethics to the social character and essence of the one new man. The hostility produced, for example, by historic, social, racial differences is destroyed. An unheard-of peace between all individuals or groups is established. Now they need and meet one another in common worship and love: "In one Spirit we both have access to the Father" (2:18). ". . . love is the fulfilling of the law" (Rom. 13:10).

But why does Paul speak of "one new man" when the essence of this man is "peace" between at least *two* persons and their common peace with God (cf. Rom. 5:1-11)? The next parallel and the best explanation is found in Ephesians 5:31. When a man has left father and mother and is joined to his wife "the two shall become *one* flesh," "*one* body" (cf. 1 Cor. 6:16). Paul quotes this passage from Genesis 2 in order to elucidate both Christ's relation to the church and the husband's relation to his wife (Eph. 5:21-33). Though in this context he does not speak of the interrelation of Jews and Gentiles, we may learn from the text that the "one body" of Christ[15] is not an amalgamation of the Son of God with man, but denotes Christ's dominion, redemptive love, partnership, and the church's submission, bridal fidelity, participation in his goodness. The specific mutual attachment of bridegroom and bride, rather than the wiping out or denial of differences, is essential to the life of this body. The same is true of marriage. The "one flesh" or the "one body" to which husband and wife are joined is not a super-, neuter-, or standard-man, but the reality of peace and love between two different persons. Their individual characteristics are far from being wiped out. Precisely the union of their differences is decisive.

The "new" man is wearing neither a uniform nor crutches. He is not made a hermaphrodite or a hybrid. He is neither a rampant individualist nor a pious individual nor an anonymous and unstructured collective. He is not the result of different ingredients or functions, but he lives in the communion of different persons. In the body of Christ the differences between its manifold members are as little abrogated as is the distinction of the one Son of God from the many saints. But the specific dignity and responsibility of each partner is recognized and comes alive precisely in their mutual coordination.

The great example, the test of unity in difference and of distinctiveness in unity, is the common life of Jews and Gentiles under the gospel. According to Ephesians 2:15 and 3:6, the Gentiles became members of the one body of Christ only by their insertion into Israel. According to 2:21 f. and 4:16, they remain and grow in the same structure only as they continue to be "joined together," "built in," "knit together." Precisely when Jews and Gentiles are united their mutual but distinctive responsibility is awakened and becomes actual and urgent. The church is the bride of Christ only when it is the church of Jews and Gentiles.

Much ought to be said about the means by which the peace between the former enemies was made, the wall broken down, the division of the law abrogated, the church founded. The central passage of Ephesians, i.e., 2:11-22, makes it unmistakably clear that there was neither a superior quality inherent in Israel which made this people able to absorb the Gentiles in the unity of the people of God, nor a hitherto hidden superiority of the Gentiles which forced Israel to open her gates to the outsiders. According to Ephesians 2:13-17, nothing but the mediation of the Messiah made the difference. "*Through him* both of us have in one Spirit access to the Father" (Eph. 2:18). Had Israel not been given the promised Messiah, had this Messiah not officiated as high priest and suffered as victim at the same time (Eph. 2:17, 5:2), were he not his own proclaimant, were he no longer present and at work in the Spirit—the one new man, the church of Jews and Gentiles, would not live. Without the "Savior" and his "love" there would be no "body" of those sanctified and united (cf. Eph. 5:23, 25-27). But a more detailed description of the manner by which and the price at which the church was founded and is being built will be given in the next section. At this point our concern is merely with the result of Christ's death and the Spirit's operation—an effect identified with the peace between Jews and Gentiles to be epitomized by the church.

What happens to Israel after the Gentiles have been brought in by Israel's Messiah? Is Israel now to be preached bad news (just as early prophets in Israel pronounced the Gentiles' doom) because Paul received the task to preach the good news of the Son among the nations (Gal. 1:16)? The divided and hostile human race's reconciliation with God and among one another, and the emergence of the church from the Jews and the Gentiles, do not mean that because of Christ the Gentiles are "in," whereas the Jews are "out." "He preached peace to you who were far off *and* to those who were near" (Eph. 2:17). Reconciliation means that all hostility has come to an end. Together the old and the new citizens, the ingrown and the newly accepted members, have access to the Father (2:18 f.). Thus the existence, building, and growth of the church are identified with the common existence, structure, and growth of Jews and Gentiles.

The manifold tensions between Christians and Jews—some openly admitted, some hidden or repressed—cannot obliterate the peace brought by Jesus the Messiah. The Messianic peace is a reality despite human incomprehension, denial, rebellion against it. Under no circumstances should the word "peace" be spiritualized or otherwise devalued. It does not mean "peace of mind," "acceptance of being accepted," "relief of anxiety." But just as in the Old Testament, in Ephesians too this word has a social and universal (also material) meaning. In Ephesians 2:14-15 peace with Israel is a peace which is inseparable from peace with God (2:16-18). All evidence may speak against it; war and war cries, incrimination and suspicion, may find their expression even within the walls of the church and between the covers of theological books—but this peace that was made and proclaimed by Christ is not to be undone. Some misled soldiers may continue warring long after the conclusion of peace. They deprive themselves and others of the fruits of peace. Yet the peace already concluded is real and valid.

Ephesians 3:5-6 confirms and augments the weight of points made earlier. "In other generations the secret of Christ was not made known to the sons of men as it has now been revealed through the Spirit to his holy apostles and prophets. (It was revealed now only) that the Gentiles are fellow heirs, members of the same body, fellow partakers of the promises (of God) in Christ Jesus."

According to these verses the formerly hidden "dispensation" (3:2, 1:10, 3:9), that is, God's "wisdom," "purpose" (3:10 f.), or "secret" (3:3 f. and 9) have but one content and meaning: the adoption of Gentiles into rights equal with those enjoyed by the Jews, and the ensuing coalescence of the Gentiles into one body, brotherhood, and covenant life together with Israel.

Brotherhood with Israel is therefore in Ephesians not just a possible or desirable consequence of the eternal plan of God, of the making of peace through the cross of Christ, and of the revelation of his mystery through the Spirit. What God has planned, performed, and revealed has no other content and character than precisely this full community of the Gentiles with Israel. Brotherhood with Israel is the very essence, not the possible consequence, of the peace Christ has made. Ephesians is outstanding among the Pauline epistles because of the number of daring combinations of the Greek preposition *syn* ("with," "together with," "same") with nouns and verbs (2:19-22; 3:6; 4:3, 16). Except in 2:5-6, where obviously the resurrection and enthronement "with Christ" are meant (and except in Greek idiomatic words occurring in 5:7, 11; 3:4; 5:17), these combinations all appear to refer to the oneness, the one new man, created by Christ out of Gentiles and Jews.

While in our time the communal, relational, corporate nature of conversion, repentance, service, witness, is widely emphasized, one thing may be overlooked even by some of the most ardent promoters of the common life of Christians: the importance of the church's common life with Israel and the Christians' common life with the Jews. When in Galatians 3:28, Colossians 3:11, 1 Corinthians 12:13, Paul speaks of the oneness in Christ which supersedes national, social, cultural, racial distinctions, he always begins his enumeration of the previously inimical camps with reference to "Jew and Greek" or "Jews and Greeks." The gospel he preaches and the missionary way he follows (according to Luke's account in Acts) always demonstrate the priority of Israel: "the Jew first, and the Greek (or, Gentile)" are addressed and visited by him.[16]

What is true of Paul's preaching and missionary tactics holds also true of his ethics. In Romans 12 and thereafter, ethical questions are treated only after (in chapters 9-11) the relation be-

tween the church and Israel is extensively discussed. In Philippians 3:17-4:9 the readers of this letter are called to become
Paul's imitators and to ponder whatever is true, honorable, just,
virtuous, and laudable only after, in 3:2-16, they have been made
to look at those "who mutilate the flesh" and upon Paul's own
Hebrew past. Similarly, in Ephesians the ethical appeals concerning peace and love among God's children[17] follow upon the
description of that peace which God in his love and his beloved
son created between the Gentiles and Israel (2:1-22).

This structure of Paul's argument reveals that Paul did not
sit back after stating that God has elected "first the Jews, and
(then) the Gentiles." Instead, Paul himself follows God's procedure, and he exhorts the churches to do the same (Eph. 5:1). What
it means to have, as far as possible, peace with all men—with the
brothers and the enemy, with believers and unbelievers, with
weak and strong characters (Rom. 12-15)—all of this will be
learned, tested, shown in the Christians' conversation with Israel.

Understanding and acceptance of this preference given to Israel would seem to be easy, if in Ephesians 2:12 the meaning of
the term "Israel" were only restricted. With which Israel have
the Gentiles been united through the peace made by Christ? If
merely ancient Israel were meant, even that Israel which was
promised God's Messiah;[18] or if Paul thought only of the rem-
nant of Israel as represented in the Gospels by the disciples of
Jesus[19] and others; or if Paul had in mind only individual true
worshipers in spirit and in truth like Nathanael, the Israelite in
whom there is nothing false[20]—then a noble selection from Israel, not the totality of the Jewish people and history, would be
partners of the Gentiles in the peace and worship established by
Christ. Such an Israel and such Israelites might be placed before
the readers of Paul's letters who are heroes of faith. With them it
would be natural and easy to enjoy company. But Paul's argument is not so simple, moralistic, idealistic, cheap. In other letters he speaks more often of the "Jews" than of "Israelites," and
of "the circumcision" rather than of the obedient Jewish children
or servants of God. Once he gives a bitter description of what
"the Jews" did and do (1 Thess. 2:14-16). Bitingly, he criticizes

what he calls man's (or self-) righteousness.[21] In a warm tone he speaks of his intercession for his "kinsmen by race" (Rom. 9:1 ff.). In all these cases he displays a realism that has nothing to do with idealistic or religious hero worship.

Actually, the "Israel" of which Paul speaks in Ephesians is not only that part of Israel which confesses Jesus the Messiah. It is Israel in every possible definition of that term. A distinction between Israel and Israel, as made in Romans 9:6 ("not all who are descended from Israel belong to Israel"), is not made. Those given the promise and those who always murmur against God; those given the Messiah and those who crucify or (like Paul himself) persecute God's anointed, the gospel, and the church; those of the past and their fleshly and spiritual children in the present —Paul means all of them. Today the young state of Israel ought to be included as much as the Jews living in dispersion all over the world. When in Ephesians Paul speaks of those calling themselves the circumcision (2:11), he shows that he does not exclude moralistic or pharisaic or orthodox heretical Judaism from his concept of the "commonwealth of Israel" (2:12). Indeed, according to Acts (18:19-20:21), a synagogue, the learned Apollos, the disciples of John, sons of a high priest, migrating (Jewish) exorcists, and—according to Revelation 2:2—so-called (Jewish) apostles, all were found in Ephesus. Whether Ephesians was originally addressed to Ephesus only or to many or all of the Asia Minor churches, Jews of all kinds lived around, among, in harmony or in discord with, the Christians here addressed. What Paul writes (Eph. 2:14-18) about the peace between those far and those near and about the common access of Jew and Gentile to God, concerns the Christians' relationship to the actual Israel, not to an idealized Israel. In speaking of the "one new man" created by God in Christ (Eph. 2:15), Paul thinks of both Jews and Gentiles just as they are. "We (the Jews) did the will of the flesh . . . and were by nature children of wrath like the others (that is, the Gentiles)" (Eph. 2:3). Christ did not die for angels but for men. The men for whom he died were sinners and enemies (Rom. 5:6-10). The Jews and Gentiles united by Christ were not an elite from both groups but a beginning that was and is representative of the whole mass of all mankind. Therefore, the message of Ephesians must not be so curtailed as to be reduced to a message concerning Jewish- and Gentile-born *Christians* only.

C. UNITY THROUGH THE MESSIAH

We now ask for the reasons which Paul gives for his surprising way of describing the church's relation to Israel. There are some seemingly respectable reasons he fails to proffer.

He does not argue on a general, enlightened humanitarian line, saying, "All men are ultimately equal; so let us forget religious, cultural, racial, historical differences!" Paul does not use this kind of proposition in any of his letters. Whether he characterizes man as a sinner or a saint, he always pictures him in his relationship to God; he thinks only in this relationship.

Also Paul does not think like a professor of the history of religions or make merely an emotional application of cultural facts or insights. He never makes use of an argument current in our days, saying, "Our Christian religion is mainly derived from the Hebrew religion, even though to its own good or harm it has agglomerated elements of Gentile diction, imagery, liturgy, and style of life. We Christians, therefore, owe the Jews a historical, cultural, and moral debt, and must not deny or despise the Hebrew patrimony but acknowledge it and prove thankful for it in the interest of Christian integrity." Occasionally Paul did not refrain from radical breaks with the time-honored Jewish tradition and highly respected authorities. Also when he preached Christ, he was concerned with more than the preservation of memorials to Christian origins. His concern was with living people, not with cultural values as such.

Except for the biting and bitter statements about the Jews found in 1 Thessalonians 2:14-16, Paul's attitude toward his Jewish brothers is distinguished by humanity. He showed gratitude for the promise, the directives, the liturgical traditions which they kept. He was not blind to the relevance of continued Jewish existence, however hard the hardening of the Jewish hearts and the punishments and sufferings inflicted on them. He cared and did not give up hope for Israel. He was no less exasperated than any one of Israel's prophets by what he saw happening in his people. He had to cry out against wrong judgments and deeds. But in his heart and thought he remained faithful to Israel. Recent research in the Pauline corpus has shown how closely Paul's teaching was related to Jewish wisdom literature, to the orthodox rabbinical thought, but sometimes also to sectarian, apocalyptic, and apocryphical teaching. Paul's dependency upon the Old Testament and upon official and heterodox Judaism is visible in the abundance of Scripture quotations, in the content and manner of his exegetical discourses, in his terminology, and especially in his conviction that the age of the Messiah changes all and everything. It is not in vain that he calls Jesus "the Messiah," the annointed king given by God to Israel. Still, the mere fact and fashion of Paul's undeniably close, grateful, and alert relation to Jewish tradition of various types is not, as such, the reason for the relatedness of Gentiles and Jews to which he bore witness.

Throughout Ephesians and similarly in other epistles, the unique reason which Paul gives for his teaching of the Christians' and the Jews' coexistence as fellow citizens and brothers is summed up in the two words "in Christ." The hymn of Ephesians 1:3-10 which praises God for his eternal will that now has come to pass is dominated by these two words. The ethics of the *Haustafeln* (5:21-6:9) is determined by them. Between these passages is found the description of God's work of redemption and revelation (Eph. 2-3). Especially in 2:13-22 explicit reference to Christ is made in ever new variations.

Paul tells what has become of the Gentiles "in Christ." In *the blood of Christ* they have been brought near. *Christ* is our (i.e., the Jews' and the Gentiles') peace; *he* made out of the two one . . . *in his flesh . . . in himself . . . in one body . . . through the cross . . . in himself. He* came and preached peace . . . *through him* we have access . . . *in one Spirit.* The cornerstone or capstone is *"Jesus Christ in whom* the whole structure is joined together and grows into a holy temple *in the Lord, in whom* you also are built together."* Correspondingly, the Gentiles' previous exclusion, hopelessness, and godlessness are attributed to the fact that "at that time they were *without Christ*." Finally, according to Ephesians 3:4-6, the Gentiles are fellow heirs, members of the same body, fellow participants in the promise, according to "the mystery of *Christ*," and "*in Jesus Christ* through the gospel."

Paul appears indefatigable in his repeated references to Christ. However, the words "in Christ," "in him," and the equivalent expressions "in his flesh, blood, cross" can hardly be considered as mechanical repetitions of liturgical formulations. For fear of killing them, a reasonable liturgist would never overdo the use of such important formulae.

The name "Christ (Jesus)" is interpreted in two different ways that emphasize Christ's unique past and his ongoing, unfulfilled personal work respectively. On the one side Jesus Christ's sacrificial death is stressed. To this end classical concepts of sacrifice, such as "blood . . . flesh . . . body" (2:13-16), are used as well as novel terms which only apply to Christ's sacrifice, such as "cross" and "Spirit."[22] On the other side the work of the Spirit, i.e., the revelation of Christ's mystery and the preaching of the gospel (2:17, 3:4-6), are pointed out. The death of Christ, the preaching of peace, and the self-revelation of the resurrected Christ to and through appointed witnesses (3:1 ff.; 4:7 ff.)—these facts constitute the reason Paul gives for the solidarity of Jews and Gentiles. These events are founded in God's eternal love for Christ and the eternal election of the saints (1:4-10).

Christ crucified, revealed, and at work in his proclamation— he alone is the founder, the mover, and the shaper of the church created from Jews and Gentiles. How very Pauline this argument is, may be elucidated by reference to 1 Corinthians 1:18-24: "the word of the cross . . . the power of God . . . we preach Christ crucified . . . to those who are called, both Jews and Greeks, Christ the power of God and the wisdom of God." Also in Romans 1:16 the gospel is designated as God's power of salvation for every one who believes, the Jews and also the Gentiles.

The Greek word "Christ," in most passages of the New Testament where it occurs, should be translated by "the Messiah." The crucified "King of the Jews" is the one who preaches peace and who is proclaimed by his servants. The sum of *his* work and *his* death, the contents of *his* proclamation (2:17) and *his* revealed mystery are this: Jews and Gentiles are now "created (to be) one new man" (2:15). The unification of Jews and Gentiles, therefore, is not the result of humanitarian thought or of some yearning for a lost paradise. Rather it is attributed to God's good pleasure alone. It is warranted through the mystery of Christ, fulfilled on the cross and revealed through the Spirit (3:4, 7; 2:16, 18; cf. Rom. 11:25-36). Husband and wife may become one flesh without the mentioning of Christ's name, many a sexual union may belie the union with Christ (1 Cor. 6:13-20), but Jews and Gentiles are united and become one "in Christ" only. Through him alone they are made members of one and the same body, *his body* (1:23, 2:15, 3:6).

The Christological center of Paul's message reveals that he is a pragmatist rather than a dreaming idealist. Paul bases his statements upon what happened on the cross and what is revealed by the Spirit. In his death the King of the Jews took the sides of both camps, by standing in the breach (cf. Ps. 106:23)—or rather by destroying the wall between them (Eph. 2:14). According to an ancient interpretation quoted by Irenaeus, Christ stretched his hands to both enemies. His sacrifice was accepted as a "fragrant offering" (Eph. 5:2). The Jews who were dead in sins (Eph. 2:1, 5) and "by nature children of wrath, like the rest of mankind" (Eph. 2:3) needed resurrection as much as the Gentiles. Together with the Gentiles they were resurrected "in Christ" (Eph. 2:5-6). The Gentile-born Christians must not forget but "remember" (Eph. 2:11) that all which they were given from God was only given to them together with Israel and for the purpose of their being together. They cannot be joined or built, nor can they grow into God's holy temple unless they recognize that this joining, building, growing happens only together with Israel. This implies fellow citizenship in the same commonwealth, and brotherhood in the same house. The prodigal would not have come home unless he had returned to the father who loved the older brother as much as the younger and unless he had come into that house to which the older brother had always belonged and into which he was still implored to reenter. If it were not for Christ, the King of the Jews, an exclusive relationship between Gentile Christians and God might be dreamed of. "In the Messiah," however, it is impossible to claim or to enjoy any communion with God which does not include the Jews.

The enterprise of promoting, forming, and maintaining separate Judaeo-Christian theologies and congregations is excluded by the Christocentric heart of Paul's argument. If special words are addressed separately to Jewish and Gentile Christians, and the troubles and hopes of certain groups are given special consideration, then there is yet no invitation to build new walls or retain old fences of separation. Equally excluded, of course, is the discrimination against individual Judaeo-Christians belonging to a predominantly Gentile Christian congregation.

A second consequence should perhaps have been mentioned first. The Jews who do not yet know or acknowledge what has happened "in the Messiah" may resemble the older brother who, in the parable, keeps apart. But precisely these Jews—as much as baptized Jews—are brothers of the Christians. Unless Gentile Christians respect and love them, they deny God's election. Nobody but the prodigal should be more aware of what it means to stand outside, to murmur, and to resent the generous and liberating love of the Father. To live in enjoyment of this love—as the Ephesians do (1:4, 2:4-5, 5:1, etc.)—means to acknowledge the indefatigability and irresistibility of God's love. Because of God's love Israel has an indelible character as God's firstborn. The faithlessness of Israel cannot nullify God's faithfulness (Rom. 3:3-4). ". . . has God rejected his people? By no means!" (Rom. 11:1). ". . . do not become proud, but stand in awe" (Rom. 11:20). This is the meaning of the words "in the Messiah." It is to their own detriment that Gentile-born Christians neglect this faithfulness. It is fine to sing, "In Christ there is no East and West." But the sincerity of such hymns will be tested by the witness of our lives. We are called to testify that "in Christ" the church is one, holy, apostolic, and catholic only when she lives in solidarity with the Jews. The "communion of the saints" which is confessed in the Apostles' Creed is interpreted by Ephesians 2:19 as communion with Israel. In the Old as well as the New Testament the saints are sinners called into unity with God and to the service of God.

D. THEOLOGICAL IMPLICATIONS

Before we attempt to say more, in a final part, about the practical consequences of the teaching in Ephesians on the church and Israel, we have to outline the theological implications contained in the specific message of Ephesians. No lesser issues than the doctrine of God, the doctrine of man, and the doctrine of the church are at stake when the church's relationship to Israel is considered.

1. *That God is faithful* and that man has good reasons to trust his faithfulness (Rom. 3:3-4, 1 Cor. 10:13, etc.)—these are the first things demonstrated by what Paul writes about the church and Israel. In Ephesians the term "faithful" is not used as an attribute of God. We use it here as a summary description of what Paul is saying[23] about God's promise and about the eternity, solidity, and performance of God's will, counsel, and plan. If God is "one,"[24] then this confession asserts not only his numerical oneness. It includes also the praise of his consistency with himself.

If election, grace, covenants, promises, fathership of God, building of a house had come into being only with the Gentile-born Ephesians' conversion and gathering, then we could not possibly know and show that the eternal will (Eph. 3:11) and plan of God was and is carried out by the inclusion of Gentiles into God's people. God might be imagined to be an arbitrary god who has deigned, in some sudden good mood, to make the Ephesians feel happy as his children and as heirs of heavenly riches. Nothing could prevent them, or their Jewish and Gentile critics, from suspecting or fearing that God's mood might change again or that all their "faith" was but wishful thinking! But Paul wants to remind them that they were chosen, gathered, built up, sealed according to the eternal election and economy of God—so much so that there is no danger of God's going back on his manifest will. In order to do so, Paul refers to a plan of God conceived outside of time (Eph. 1:4, 3:11).

Paul's main argument, however, is not that God's decree and manifestation are timeless or above time. Rather, his point is to show that grace, election, covenants, the building of the house of God on earth did not begin with the Ephesians. By election they were inserted into a preexisting community, commonwealth, and house. They were made participants in a heritage, a unity, a promise already given. What preexists, according to Ephesians, is not a blueprint to be carried out in history. What precedes the Ephesians' calling is Israel's election to be God's people. God did not become Father by calling the Ephesians his children. But all fatherhood in heaven and upon earth is derived from him (Eph. 2:12, 19; 3:15). The kingship of God is not an idea that started with the Gentile Christians, but the demonstration of the power and riches of God and the building of a commonwealth preceded their reception into citizenship. God did not change when he acted according to his "good pleasure" (Eph. 1:5, 9, K.J.V.). Even what was done "in Christ" manifested nothing but what was eternally resolved in Christ.

So God was faithful to himself when he adopted the Gentiles. Without looking upon Israel, the Ephesian Christians might be doubtful about the solidity and permanence of God's plan and work with them. The reference to Israel serves almost as reference to a proof not only of God's existence but also of God's character, that is, of his faithfulness. If we leave Israel out of the preaching of Jesus Christ, we are left with intellectualistic, idealistic, or emotionalistic religion. The identity of God, whom the Gentile-born saints call Father in the name of Jesus the Messiah, is manifested to and for them only by Israel.

2. *That man is saved by grace alone* (Eph. 2:5, 8) is equally a fact which can be demonstrated and acknowledged only when the Christian's solidarity with Israel is observed. The preexistence of a commonwealth and house, of a plan, of covenants and promises of God in the history of Israel reminds the Gentiles to look at their own history and to appreciate that only by sheer grace they are no longer dead in sins and strangers (2:5, 8, 12, 19).

They received privileges first granted to others. The stranger has no right to enjoy the peace of a house—especially when his heart is hardened, his way foolish, his intention greedy as that of the Gentiles described in Ephesians 4:17-19. According to Ephesians 2:3-12, the saints in Ephesus had been exactly such Gentiles; Ephesians 4:17 and 5:3-12 show how great their temptation was to slide back to their origin. The existence of Jews at their side, in their midst, and around them makes them remember how undeserved was God's grace, how deadly their fall and plight.

But even more, by looking at Jews the Gentiles realize which kind of man is confronted by God: Man is a sinner. This is why every Gentile is by nature an anti-Semite. The images of the grim Mordecai and the weeping Jeremiah; of the shrewd Jacob and the complaining Job; of the ceremonious Aaron and the punctilious scribe Ezra; of assimilation-happy Sadducees and their zealot and pharisaical antagonists; of the Jew, Matthew, and Gamaliel's ex-pupil, Paul; of the people of Israel as a whole as well as of its individual representatives, including the King of the Jews at the cross—they are all basically repulsive to the Greek mind. The attempts of a Philo and Josephus to demonstrate the opposite only give evidence to the same fact. The Jews were not the kind of philosophers and artists that are approved and respected by Greek academies. Their service in the midst of the nations differs from the service that eminent Gentiles have rendered to mankind. Israel is, first of all, God's servant among and to mankind, regardless of whether she agrees to this service or not or whether this service makes her popular or unpopular. Yet, in the Israelite type of servanthood there is—as a classic Jewish author has stated in unsurpassable words—"no form or comeliness that we should look at him, and no beauty that we should desire him . . . his appearance was so marred beyond human semblance, and his form beyond that of the sons of men" (Isa. 53:2, 52:14). "Who is blind but my servant, or deaf as my messenger whom I send?" (Isa. 42:19). Exodus 1:18-22, not to speak of Esther 3:7-15, reads like a manifesto of the reasons and methods of anti-Semitism. Nobody among the Gentiles likes the picture of mankind which is presented by the Jews: elect and yet murmuring, redeemed and yet rebellious, gifted and yet squandering, privileged by unsurpassed grace and yet relying upon righteousness by their own works.

By kicking at and killing the Jews, the Gentiles have always attempted to avert from themselves that mirror of man's face which is so disreputable in effect. There is no one among them who would not believe himself to be at least in part a man better than the Jew. There is no one who is not embarrassed, like a thief caught in the act, by the presence of the Jew in his environment. The Jew reminds him, simply by his presence, of sins he does not like to admit, of guilt in the past and helplessness in the present. Above all, the Gentile will not believe that this Jewish people should represent God's favored and chosen. How could he—as long as he denies his solidarity with the servant people who have nothing to show but their unworthiness and yet live by the grace of his Lord? As in Paul's time, such logic is folly to natural man. All pogroms and all secret stabs at the Jewish fellowman are only attempts to overcome the disturbance made by such a man and such a God. "How odd of God—to choose the Jews!"

The Jews are the most sensible and touchy point of both God's and man's life. Probably for this reason they are compared with the "eyeball" of both God and mankind: God kept Jacob "as the apple of his eye" (Deut. 32:10); "Keep me as the apple of the eye" (Ps. 17:8); ". . . he who touches you touches the apple of his eye" (Zech. 2:8). So the Jews reveal what a surprising God the Lord is, and what an amazing action is the salvation of man by God. If, despite their mutterings and rebellion, the Jews' salvation is the type and exemplar of man's salvation, then nothing is left but to say that we are saved by grace (Eph. 2:5, 8). Anti-Semitism—whether in churchly or pagan form—is therefore always a display of work-righteousness and self-redemption. Only those Christians who in deeds, sufferings, and words reveal their own full share in the guilt and the plight of the Jews give a testimony to their faith in salvation by grace alone.

3. *That childhood in the father's house is solidarity with those fellowmen who are hard to bear*—this is another factor evidenced by the Christians' being joined and built together with Israel.

Upon the ground of very general exegetical and historical, psychological and sociological, analyses it can easily be shown why it is better to pray "Our Father" than "My Father." Religion without community, faith without tradition from fathers, devotion without cultus have indeed a bad press among twentieth-century religious and secular writers. But how can we know that the celebrated *koinonia* and *diakonia* (that is, "fellowship," "community," "sharing," "living in relationship," "participation") are anything better than welcome means to make the individual (that is, the so-called "integrated personality") the goal and end of all man's ways? Why should the worship of collectivism—as displayed in academic exegetical quarters by the form-critical school, in educational quarters by group dynamics, in political quarters by the formation of Eastern and Western blocs—reveal a real alternative to the superego, which the last century celebrated with its worship of the genius, the princes and presidents, Queen Victoria, and the infallible pope?

According to Ephesians there is only one criterion to show whether Christians are honest in acknowledging that they need their fellowman in order to have access to God. This criterion is their solidarity with the Jews. To recognize that Jesus Christ is *their* king before he is *ours;* that the Holy Writings were theirs before they also became ours; that the Jews, despite dispersion, persecution, and mass murder, were and are kept alive by God's grace; that their toiling and working in the Father's house is what we prodigals should have done—to accept all this is not only fitting but necessary for Christians. The Jew is the fellowman par excellence—not because Gentiles have chosen him, but because they have become children of God, only by having been made *his* fellowmen. Should the Christians deny their brotherhood with Israel—their solidarity with all Jews—they would by the same token exclude themselves from the household of God. When the prodigal finds the way to his older brother, he also will have an open door to every other man. Unless he recognizes in full and deep solidarity the pangs through which that brother has to go, his sympathy for the woes and joys of other fellowmen will be shallow.

The Christians are made, by Jesus Christ, fellow citizens and fellow heirs with the Jews rather than with anybody else, in order that they may see and know that God elected grumbling, murmuring sinners. It was God's "pleasure" (Eph. 1:5, 9, K.J.V.) to elect the "brothers" who always attempt to stay outside, although their place should be inside where forgiveness is celebrated. It pleased him to choose the men who consider themselves the only insiders, although they should humbly recognize that in their grumbling they refuse to give the glory to God the Father. The brotherhood which constitutes the church is not the easygoing chumminess of members of a saintly club. Neither is it the historical, emotional, or strategic alliance of the world's best people. Such brotherhood is the common life, the solidarity of sinners who recognize how much greater than abounding sin is God's overabundant grace (Rom. 5:15-21, 11:32).

Fellowship in the church is fellowship with the man who may believe he has the right to grumble, kick, and swear at his fellowman and who certainly is not innocent in doing so. It is comradeship with the brother who has something against you (Matt. 5:23)—and not only with the brother against whom we may bear some grudge. The ethical part of Ephesians, especially the generalizing statements about unity, kindness, submission (4:3, 32; 5:21) show as clearly as the antitheses of the Sermon on the Mount (Matt. 5:21-48) the nature of brotherhood and love. As long as we love those who love us, we are no different from other sinners (Matt. 5:43-48). If "the communion of the saints" is community, fellow citizenship in a kingdom and fellow membership in a household with the sometimes odd "saints" of Israel, then the behavior of the church toward the Jews is not a question of opinion or opportunism but rather a criterion of the Christians' faith, love, and hope.

E. PRACTICAL APPLICATIONS

We conclude with a look at only three of the many practical consequences that follow from the specific relationship between Israel and the church. These three points appear of special interest to Gentile Christians today and, though not explicitly treated in Ephesians, are illumined greatly by this epistle.

1. *The Use of the Scriptures.* Because in Ephesians 3:5, 4:11, and elsewhere Paul speaks of "prophets" living within the Christian church, it is probable that the "foundation of the apostles and prophets" upon which the church is built (Eph. 2: 20) is the foundation of the chief New Testament ministers of God. But a strong group of interpreters still holds that the New Testament apostles are combined with Old Testament prophets.[25] Whichever interpretation is chosen, the whole context of Ephesians 2:20, especially Ephesians 2:11-22 and 3:1-6, deals with the church's relationship to Israel and with the relationship of Jews and Gentiles within the church. It has often been said that references to the Old Testament in sermons (like those contained in Acts), in narrative and doctrinary documents (as in the Gospels and Epistles of the New Testament), and in brief confessional formulations (as in 1 Corinthians 15:3 f.) were primarily to be considered as an apologetic device used by early Christian preachers and teachers (and aimed in part at Jews, in part at Gentiles) to undergird, if not prove, their statements about the person and work of Jesus Christ and about the eschatological character of the church. It has become customary to speak somewhat despicably of the "Scripture proofs" and of the rather suspicious methods of interpretation which are employed to "prove" a given point.

However, this negative appraisal of the New Testament passages dealing with the fulfillment of what is "written . . . in the law of Moses and the prophets and the psalms" (Luke 24:44) hardly renders justice to the weight and intention the quoted passages have in the writings of Paul, Matthew, Luke, 1 Peter, and the author of Hebrews. If community with Israel is essential and basic to the church's foundation, life, and order, then references to the fulfillment of the Old Testament are not primarily an academic or literary trick comparable to the footnote strategy which lends a very learned though not always equally persuasive character to some theological literature of our time. In the New Testament, Scripture quotations and allusions belong to the very core of the matter that is announced. They are proclamation and exhortation rather than mere reasonings; they deal with the fulfillment of the Old Covenant, not with reflections about an old book. We hold that originally the early Christian speakers and authors quoted and explained the Old Testament because they wanted to inculcate the brotherhood and solidarity of Israel and the church. Is Paul's doctrine of justification by faith the invention of a genius, an ingenious exploitation of the cross and resurrection? By no means! Abraham was justified by faith—and "So shall your descendants be" (Rom. 4:18)! Is the conflict between flesh and spirit, the suffering of the present time, and the hope for perfection only an imitation of decadent, Hellenistic self-pity? Not by far! Israel's past, present, and future is nothing else but justification and glorification by grace alone (Rom. 7-11). Is Paul the first to value God's promise higher than God's law? Nonsense! The covenant with Abraham was made before the covenant of Sinai, and the giving of the law was preceded by the promise of God and followed by the fulfillment of promise (Gal. 3-4).

It is, however, rather obvious that Barnabas and Justin Martyr mostly cite the Old Testament for reasons other than to comfort and warn the Christians by referring to their solidarity with Israel. Marcion's and his Gnostic brethren's rejection of the Old Testament may be explained as a reaction against a trite apologetic exploitation of those books. The majority of the New Testament writers, however, do not suffer from pseudo-Christian superiority complexes over against Israel, nor do they believe in using cheap, apologetic propaganda methods which began to abound in some of the orthodox, but also in heterodox second-century literature. Much more they study, use, and quote the Old Testament happily and frequently because they apparently know no other way to learn and to describe the identity and faithfulness of God, sinful man's reconciliation by sheer grace, and the common life of those called to be saints. That *this* God was in Christ reconciling *this* man to enjoy *such* life—these propositions, it appears, they could only proclaim with the help of the Old Testament.

Explicit Old Testament quotations or allusions may be missing in some documents (so in 1 Thessalonians, Philemon, and the Epistles of John); but the great majority of New Testament books show that the good news of Jesus the Messiah cannot be told without reference to the Old Testament—without the testimony to Israel's election, life, worship, hope. The magnificent confession, "One Father ... one Lord ... one Spirit ... one body ... one faith ... one hope" (see Ephesians 4:4-6) is founded upon the renewal of the promised Covenant, which became real in Jesus Christ's coming, death, and rule.

2. *The Conversion of Israel.* According to Acts 20:21, Paul gave testimony "to Jews and to Greeks" in Ephesus, and there are no reasons to doubt the accuracy of this statement. However, as was mentioned above, Ephesians is addressed to Gentile Christians only. Should this prove that the author of Ephesians had given up hope for the Jews—the hope that the veil would be lifted from their reading of the Scripture (2 Cor. 3:15-16; Acts 28:15-28)? Or did he intend to leave for good the "gospel to the circumcised" to Peter, James, and John (Gal. 2:7-9)? Or did he carry out a preconceived plan to "make Israel jealous" (Rom. 11:11-14) by a full "turn to the Gentiles" (Acts 13:46) and by a corresponding neglect of the Jews? Indeed, many Christian churches have at times behaved as if mission to the Gentiles alone were the order of the day, as if the church did not owe any testimony to the Jews anymore. But statements like Romans 9:3 and 11:14 indicate clearly how much Paul cared for the salvation of his people: Paul would gladly take upon himself God's rejection if thereby he could "save some" of his brothers according to the flesh.

In Ephesians we do find a statement about the unity of faith and knowledge of God's Son to which "all" should be brought through the ministry of the preachers and teachers of God's word (4:11-13). There is also an appeal to all readers to be witnesses for Christ in the world, "having shod (their) feet with the equipment of the gospel of peace" (6:15), and to intercede for the evangelizing apostle (6:18-20). But we do not find in this epistle (or in any other) any decision or exhortation to engage in what is commonly called "mission to the Jews." We know too little about the development of Paul's thought and about the specific situation of the recipients of Ephesians to explain this silence. We only know that Ephesians keeps silent at a point where false eloquence at times has done great harm. "Mission to the Jews" at any rate is not the main concern of this epistle which, among all New Testament books, speaks of Israel in the most positive terms. Is there any sensible explanation of this fact?

In Exodus, Deutero-Isaiah, and the book of Jonah (to mention only some of the relevant Old Testament books) Israel herself, or a representative of the Jews, is the public demonstration of God's faithfulness and power, of his liberty and righteousness, of his mercy and will. What God's hand does to Israel happens not only for Israel's sake, but also for the sake of the Gentiles; it makes both Israel and the Gentiles be witnesses of God's plan and work. We might venture to say that Israel is God's chosen missionary to the Gentiles. This applies to a witness given in many forms. The testimony consists not only of words, but also of the blessing bestowed upon Israel and of Israel's destiny to become a blessing to all nations (Gen. 12:1-3). Israel's mission is revealed in the exemplary punishments inflicted upon Israel and her corresponding suffering. A testimony is given by the dispersion and the subsequent gathering of Israel. The mission and testimony are verified by the benefits which nations receive from Israel, as for example, Egypt from Joseph's wisdom and virtue.

We observe that Israel is God's chosen missionary whether or not she murmurs, whether or not she obeys God and enjoys doing his will, whether or not she is aware of her mission. God made it the very nature of Israel to be his showpiece and the guarantee of his grace and might among the Gentiles. If she goes against this nature, she yet has to serve God's purpose. The liberation from Egypt, which Israel accepts but grumblingly, was carried through in order that the nations might learn that God is "able" to perform his promise (Num. 14:13-19). The Babylonian Exile, which is depicted not as a mere catastrophe but as a well-deserved punishment, is the means by which Israel becomes a light to the Gentiles (Isa. 42:6, 49:6). Jonah's shameful flight did not keep this fugitive from God from being miraculously saved and, against his will, becoming for the Ninevites the tool and type of salvation by grace alone. The deliverance of Jesus into the hands of the Gentiles and the rejection of the gospel which drives the apostles to preach to the Gentiles—all these events with many voices are telling only one thing: Israel is and remains God's missionary to the Gentiles. We may apply to Israel what Paul says about himself: ". . . necessity is laid upon me. Woe to me if I do not preach the gospel! For if I do this of my own will, I have a reward; but if not of my own will, I am entrusted with a commission" (1 Cor. 9:16-17).

In view of Israel's indelible calling to serve God as the missionary to the Gentiles, the designation "(Christian) mission to the Jews" had better be dropped. The way in which it often is carried out alienates more Jews than it wins. For who could or would dare to set himself up as a missionary to and among those who by God's decision are and remain by nature his missionaries? Only where the Old Testament is not read and known enough and consequently is not taken seriously (as is the case when people speak of the "particularism of the Hebrew religion") can Israel be put in the same category as the Gentiles and treated with well-meant zeal as a missionary object. In reality, because of God's unique involvement with her, Israel is not a people like all others. Rather, all other peoples owe gratitude for the election of this people for God's service. Without the Jews they would not know of God's existence and essence. Because of the existence of this people, they cannot evade God's self-manifestation in time and space. In the light of the wrath and mercy shown to this people and to its representatives, they know that God's "mercy triumphs over judgment" (cf. James 2:13). Christ "according to the flesh" comes from Israel (Rom. 9:5).

The Gentiles have no way of making restitution to this people in their own coin for what they have received. Gentile Christians cannot claim to be mediators of God's covenant for the benefit of the Jews; they for whom Israel is a light are not Israel's light. As little as the congregations founded by Paul can pay back to the poor among the saints in Jerusalem in spiritual gifts the gift of the gospel (Rom. 15:26 f.), can Gentile Christians presume to be missionaries to the Jews. ". . . salvation is from the Jews" (John 4:22), not vice versa.

Abandonment of false pretense means all the more acknowledgment of indebtedness. If the (mainly) Gentile congregations in Macedonia, Achaia, and Rome cannot pay their debt by spiritual goods, they still can and ought to show their appreciation by a different kind of service. By material blessings, says Paul in Romans 15:27; by an anguished heart—this he shows in Romans 9:2; by letting their light shine—as is done in all acts of solidarity. But in past and present times mission to the Jews has often been carried out with fire and sword as well as with seemingly kinder and certainly more cunning means of pressure. Most of the Gentile Christian churches became guilty in confronting the Jews, because they attempted to settle their debt to them in a faulty, pretentious, and violating manner. Yet, all erroneous and infamous actions on the side of the Christians cannot deprive the Jews of their right to a specific testimony and cannot take away the special indebtedness of the Gentile Christians toward Israel. That the Law and the Prophets are fulfilled, that the dividing wall is broken down, that the good news is the same for every sinner and every nation—these facts cannot be kept secret by the Christians, for the Jews have as much right as do the Gentiles to hear of it, to experience it, to enjoy it. The gospel "is the power of God . . . to every one who has faith, to the Jew first and also to the Greek" (Rom. 1:16). The name of the Lord has to be carried "before the Gentiles and kings and the sons of Israel" (Acts 9:15).

When Paul calls himself a debtor to the Greeks and barbarians (Rom. 1:14), he calls attention to the fact that no man is converted and equipped by the Spirit only for his own sake. When Paul received grace, he received the ministry of an apostle. Grace, therefore, is inseparable from a man's calling and equipment for missionary service (Rom. 1:5). God's gift of salvation never becomes private property to be enjoyed in seclusion. Rather, it is vivification, commission, equipment for the fulfillment of a task. Thus, in all descriptions of Paul's "conversion," the point is made that Paul was not only chosen and called but at the same time was made a tool for the election of many.[26] It is essential to the receiver of the gift of grace that he was empowered to bring light to those in darkness, just as it is the essence and the power of the beatitudes to make men a "light of the world" in order that they let their light shine before men (Matt. 5:14-16). Thus, as a consequence of the grace received, they certainly are debtors to God; but they also are debtors to the world—they owe it their witness. ". . . you shall be my witnesses" (Acts 1:8). "Mission" may be an adequate concept to describe the witness owed to the Gentiles. Yet, for the witness owed to the Jews we have to find a specific concept.

To Israel the Christians are indebted as the prodigal is to his older brother. From the "Father of all" (Eph. 4:6) the Gentile Christians have received in the Messiah Jesus a right and a share in things that, according to the law, would have been only the older brother's inheritance. In this regard, too, the Christians received "salvation from the Jews." True, it is God who handed it out to them. But if we were to forget the immeasurable riches of the Father, we would have to conclude (together with the older brother) that the younger brother received festive garments, a ring, a fatted calf, and what is indicated by these symbols at the expense of the older brother. Ephesians anticipates and wards off the idea that Israel might come to harm by the adoption and naturalization of Gentiles. The Father is said to be so immensely and incredibly rich that his riches overflow and are shared by strangers and sojourners without being diminished (1:7-8, 2:7, 3:8). Israel's past, present, and future rights, therefore, are not shortened when the Gentiles are made "fellow heirs" (3:6). But the Gentiles are to "remember" (2:11) that they owe God gratitude, admiration, and respect for being accepted in the inheritance of Israel. This remembrance differs from a merely intellectual act as soon as it takes the form of lived and suffered indebtedness and gratitude, respect and solidarity with Israel. How could the younger brother pretend to be the missionary to the older? He cannot. But he owes a testimony to him—a testimony that would be characterized by modesty, by his asking for forgiveness, by his full understanding of the right, the work, even the murmuring of the older brother. Thus, "confession of indebtedness to the Jews," rather than "mission to the Jews," would be a fitting term to describe the Gentile Christians' testimony. The term "debt" is appropriate because it expresses not only the dependence of Christians on the Jews but also their undeniable guilt.

Another alternative to the "mission to the Jews" has been elaborated by the writers of the post World War II constitution of the Netherlands Reformed Church. The apostolic character of the church is described in such a way that the *Gesprek met Israel* (conversation with Israel) is mentioned side by side with, but not as a part of, the *zending* (mission) of the church to the nations (Article VIII). In 1958 the same church sent out a pastoral letter explaining the reasons for this differentiation.

What the Dutch call "Gesprek," what in French is rendered by "dialogue," what in America sometimes has been dubbed an "approach," is to be understood in the fullest sense of the term "conversation." Conversation happens where people turn toward each other (Latin: *conversatio*); where one man accompanies his partner and stays with him in serious dialogue as did the disciples walking toward Emmaus in the company of their host; where one talks as does a friend to his friend, a brother to his brother, a citizen to his fellow citizen. The presupposition to such conversation is familiarity with one another's woes and joys, patient sharing of one another's anxieties and hopes, temptations and overcoming of temptations, stable solidarity despite possible mutual disappointments and grievances. Conversation happens where no one makes any condition for friendship, where no one puts himself up as a judge—in brief, where both partners are with each other and for each other before God and man. If, trusting in the unity brought about by Christ, Christians took steps in this direction, if they began to believe more humbly and sincerely in all that the Law and the Prophets contain (instead of turning a cold shoulder or showing a wise grin to Jews and Israeli of today)—maybe then the Jews would ask them for their reasons. Only then the time might come to speak of "Jesus of Nazareth, the King of the Jews." The assembly of the World Council of Churches in Evanston (1954) was badly advised when it turned down a motion pointing toward such conversation.

Too often it was seen as the Christians' duty to preach "at" the Jews, to denounce and scold them. No respect, no reverence, was shown; no mention made of what we owe them; no acknowledgment given of our dreadful guilt against them. After all the subtle and grievous wrong that in the name of Christ and of the church has been done to the Jews throughout the centuries, the first thing to be done now certainly is *not* an act of condescension or so-called generosity on the part of us Christians. No humiliation is greater, no insult more obdurating than the pretentious behavior of him who thinks he is sure, rich, and generous. It is time we Christians realized that we are beggars not only in relation to God but also in relation to the Jews. What we ought to beg from the Jews is forgiveness—forgiveness of the same kind as the prodigal will have to ask from his older brother if ever these two brothers are to live together in the father's household. Yet, how is it in practice? "To hear the name of Christ means for us to think of pogroms"—so I was told by a member of an orthodox Jewish family. It is obvious that the conversion of the Christians and of their churches, rather than the conversion of Israel, must be the first step and basic attitude of the Christians' conversation with Israel. In that conversation Christians need to *be* forgiven, and not to assume that they can spend or spread forgiveness.

Sincere conversion of the Christians will come as a surprise to those whom so far we have tried to convert. It is the only witness to Christ which in our conversation with the Jews has any promise. When they "see your good works" they will "give glory to your Father who is in heaven" (Matt. 5:16).

The relation between Israel and the Moslem, in turn, probably is somewhat analogous to the relation between the church and Israel. Islam is not a pagan religion but a Jewish sect. According to Genesis, Ishmael is Isaac's older brother (!) and the Koran insists that the Moslem are Abraham's firstborn. The deadlock of the "mission to the Mohammedans," as well as the hopeless tension between Israeli and Arabs, urgently calls for the "coming to himself" of the younger brother. At any rate, not by "converting" others but by being converted himself may a Christian "strengthen" his brothers (cf. Luke 22:32).

3. *The Test of Humanity and Humanism.* The anti-Semitism, which in the Western world and in Russia raises its head again and again in sophisticated or primitive forms, is largely due to an inexcusable negligence on the part of the churches. If in preaching and teaching, in works and in suffering, the Christians had always realized what Paul writes in Ephesians, anti-Semitism could not have become or be considered the legitimate concomitant of reading or teaching Jesus Christ's passion story. While in that story "the man" is identified with the "King of the Jews" (John 19:5, 19) and while there the cause of all humanity is tied up with the fulfillment of righteousness by the one Jew, Jesus of Nazareth, the same story has been made the source of blatant inhumanity, even of anti-Semitism. How is this possible? The only explanation I can find is this: We Christians have assumed the role of the pharisee who thanks God that he is not like Judas or like those Jews. This certainly is no excuse. Ephesians calls us to repentance, for it excludes a concept of man based on separation and hostility between various groups of men.

That there is an "old man" and a conduct typical of that man is not contested. This old man, however, is nothing more than a worn-out garment or an ill-fitting armor; he, therefore, is to be taken off (4:22). The work of God and Christ is called the creation of a new man (4:24, 2:15, cf. 2:10). We have shown above what it means that this new man was created from two and came into being only through Christ's sacrificial death. We now have to stress that it is a man—not a plan, image, or fiction; not an angel, superman, religious or psychic man—who was created. Ephesians 2:10 describes a real man who is created "for good works, which God prepared beforehand, that we should walk in them." This man will do what is "right" . . . the will of

God ... whatever is good (6:1, 6, 8). He is to grow, to be built, to speak the truth in love, to do honest work with his hands, to lead a worthy life, and to stand.²⁷ This truly human man does not exist apart from Israel but only in unity with her. He was not developed by eugenics; he is not the result of a mechanical, biological, social, or spiritual factory of the new man. The death of the King of the Jews for all men is this man's hour of birth, and the testimony of the prophets and apostles is his birth certificate. In brief, all men, every single one of them, are in need of the Jews in order to be truly human.

Contempt for Israel and the Messiah, and the choice of a foundation different from the one sketched in Ephesians (for example, individual or collective psychology, some theory of development, or some human ideal), immediately issue in the influx and spread of some kind of inhumanity. To name only one example: Not for nothing are the segregationists of the North and of the South mostly anti-Semites. Where segregation prevails, synagogues are desecrated or destroyed. On the other hand, Negroes and Jews do not stand together in vain in the struggle for education, liberty, and human rights.

The attitude we take toward the Jews reveals whether we recognize and accept God's judgment and God's creation of true humanity or whether we prefer our own definitions and experiments to God's word and deed. The Gentile Christians of Ephesus obviously were on their way to do the latter (4:17-19). Paul is calling them, and us too, to turn toward Israel and to allow God's way to be the salvation for Israel as well as for us. The criterion for our willingness to be human as God wants us to be human consists of our conversation with Israel.

Israel demonstrates that the Kingship of God is not from this world but reaches into it. Israel shows that God demands obedience within space and time. Israel gives an example to all men by its involvement in the cause of justice, liberty, health. Israel is the God-chosen guardian against all spiritualizing and mythologizing and demythologizing of the witness of the Bible and the confessions of the church. For she is the proof that God is not ashamed, either of having created matter and time or of using history and miracles, and that, therefore, man need not be ashamed of these things either. Thus Israel gives reason for joy in men and things as they are and reason to be cautious about all idealistic plans, schemes, and systems. Israel teaches us to put the one man and the unique and specific event above all generalities. Finally Israel has been from the beginning of her existence, and still is, the symbol of the cost and value of being God's chosen people and his instrument among the nations of the world. For Israel proves that it is worth the prize to suffer defamation and persecution for the sake of God who is one. So the Jews show what a high calling it is to be both God's servant and God's child.

The young Israeli state may appear to many contemporaries to be a strange proof of God's Kingship on earth. Its uncompromising zeal may be a disturbing phenomenon to the Greek-influenced neo-Platonists and idealists. But even if everything that mankind owes to the Jews would be caricaturized by the Jews themselves or by the Gentiles, by their mere existence the Jews would yet continue to disquiet everybody else and warn them of building idealistic theories and political blocs, of inventing dream castles and easy-going ideals, or of propagating a tragic image of the world and its history. The fact remains that Gentiles and Christians come to know God's Kingship, that they can enjoy God's love for the world, and that they can be obedient to God's calling, only when they gratefully learn from and with Israel who this God is and what the nature of love, election, and service is.

Israel, then, is the test and criterion of the life and the faith of the church, of every Christian, of each man.

NOTES

---◆◆◆---

Chapter I

1. See Reinhold Niebuhr, "The Relations of Christians and Jews in Western Civilization," in *Central Conference of American Rabbis Journal,* April, 1958, pp. 18-32; idem, in *The Godly and the Ungodly* (London: Faber & Faber, 1958), pp. 86-112, especially p. 108; Paul Tillich, "The Theology of Missions," in *Christianity and Crisis* 15, 1955/61, pp. 35-38, especially p. 38, col. 1. An entirely different and much more searching and suggestive approach is in a radical form taken by André Lacocque, *La Pérennité d'Israel* (Geneva: Labor et Fides, 1964).

2. "Judaism, Scriptures, and Ecumenism," in *Scripture and Ecumenism,* ed. Leonard Swidler (Pittsburgh: Duquesne University Press, 1965), pp. 116-117.

3. Matt. 16:16; John 1:1, 20:31; Acts 9:20; Rom. 1:3-4; 1 Cor. 1:24, 30, and 12:3; John 4:42; Rev. 19:16; Mark 1:15; 2 Cor. 5:17; Gal. 1:4; 6:15; Col. 1:13, 15.

4. See especially the works of Paul Fiebig, Strack-Billerbeck, G. F. Moore and C. F. G. Montefiore. Among those who attempted to reconstruct the essence of the pharisaical movement, Leo Baeck, Israel Abrahams, T. R. Herford, Louis Finkelstein, E. A. Finkelstein, Asher Finkel are to be mentioned specifically.

5. See Leo Baeck, *Das Evangelium als Urkunde der jüdischen Glaubensgeschichte* (Berlin: Schocken, 1938), especially pp. 56 ff.; cf. Reinhold Mayer, *Christentum und Judentum in der Schau Leo Baecks* (Stuttgart: W. Kohlhammer, 1961), pp. 50-75; H. J. Schoeps, *Paul,* trans. H. Knight (Philadelphia: The Westminster Press, 1961), especially pp. 118, 153, 158, 252 ff.

6. After Adolf Deissmann, Hans Lietzmann, and Richard Reitzenstein had their day, Adolf Schlatter's commentaries brought the overdue correction; see also W. D. Davies, *Paul and Rabbinic Judaism* London: S.P.C.K., 1948); C. K. Barrett, *From First Adam to Last* (New York: Charles Scribner's Sons, 1962); *The Gospel According to St. John* (London: S.P.C.K., 1958); Aileen Guilding, *The Fourth Gospel and Jewish Worship* (Oxford: Clarendon Press, 1960). There are signs, how-

ever, showing that the very continuation of thinking in these alternatives may be misleading. For example, see C. H. Dodd, *Interpretation of the Fourth Gospel* (Cambridge: Cambridge University Press, 1954); *Historical Tradition in the Fourth Gospel* (Cambridge: Cambridge University Press, 1963); James Barr, *The Semantics of Biblical Language* (London: Oxford University Press, 1961); D. E. H. Whitely, *The Theology of St. Paul* (Philadelphia: Fortress Press, 1964), pp. 2-8.

Arnold Toynbee, *Christianity Among the Religions of the World* (New York: Charles Scribner's Sons, 1957), pp. 161 ff., appears to go far beyond Adolf von Harnack's theory of radical Hellenization of the Christian message when he describes the development of Western Christianity as a *de facto* syncretism. Paul Tillich, *Christianity and the Encounter of the World Religions* (New York: Columbia University Press, 1963), pp. 84 ff., ventures as far out as to ascribe the doctrine of the Trinity to polytheistic influence upon Christian teachers. Such views, though popular, are not necessarily true to history.

7. A classic, brief presentation of the Tübingen creed is found in F. C. Baur, *Das Christentum und die christliche Kirche I* (Tübingen: F. C. Fues, 1853), pp. 41-59.

8. Quoted by H. J. Schoeps in *The Jewish-Christian Argument*, trans. D. E. Green (New York: Holt, Rinehart and Winston, 1963), p. 155.

9. Schwarzschild, "Judaism, Scriptures, and Ecumenism," *op. cit.*, p. 118.

10. For example, Rudolf Bultmann, *Jesus and the Word*, trans. L. P. Smith and E. H. Lantero (New York: Charles Scribner's Sons, 1934); *History of the Synoptic Tradition*, trans. John Marsh (New York: Harper & Row, 1963); *Theology of the New Testament*, trans. K. Grobel (New York: Charles Scribner's Sons, Vol. 1, 1951; Vol. II, 1955).

11. Matthew 26:63-64, Luke 22:67-70; but Mark 14:62, John 4:25-26 give different information.

12. In different ways also some Rabbis spoke of a hidden Messiah, and some Jewish Apocalyptical writings announced the Messiah would die before the fullness of God's Kingship would be manifest on earth. See the Talmudic and Apocalyptic material collected by Strack-Billerbeck, *Kommentar zum Neuen Testament aus Talmud und Midrasch* (Munich: C. H. Beck, I-IV, 1922-1928), especially I, 160 f.; II, 334, 339, 488, 552; III, 315; IV, 766, 893, 967.

13. See Romans 1:5, 15:16; Galatians 1:16.

14. See Romans 10:19, 11:11; but compare 11:14.

15. See Romans 11:15, 25, 26.

16. For example, André Schwarz-Bart, *The Last of the Just* (New York: Atheneum Publishers, 1960); the novels of Elie Wiesel (New York: Holt, Rinehart and Winston). The opposite is presented by Leon Uris' popular *Exodus*. Abraham Cohen, *The Natural and the Supernatural Jew* (New York: Pantheon Books, 1962), gives an illuminating and soul-searching account of the last 200 years of Jewish discussion on the alternatives faced in consequence of the *galuth* of God's people.

17. E.g., James 1:1-3; 1 Peter 1:1, 2:21; Matt. 5:11-16.

18. The enhancement of this antithesis has become most characteristic of Lutheran theology. Among others, Emanuel Hirsch in his
comments on John 1:17 in *Das Vierte Evangelium* (Tübingen: J. C. B.
Mohr, 1936) upholds it in radical fashion and neglects obviously those
statements of the same Gospel which fight antinomianism: "If you
believed Moses, you would believe me, for he wrote of me. . . . salvation
is from the Jews. . . . scripture cannot be broken" (5:46, 4:22, 10:35,
etc.).

19. In Matthew 7:28-29, 9:8; Mark 1:27, 2:12; Luke 4:36, 5:26,
astonishment, fear, questioning, amazement over "paradoxical" experiences are mentioned. Thomas' confession, "My Lord and my God!"
(John 20:28), has a ring of ecstasy.

20. Gen. 29:35. In Romans 2:17-29 the Apostle Paul alludes to this
etymology. He understands it ultimately to mean that God will give
praise to the true Jew.

21. Cf. Rom. 1:3, Heb. 7:14, Rev. 5:5.

22. The contents of Genesis 12:1-3 are reflected in Acts 3:26;
Galatians 3:8, 9, 13, 14. Equally the message of Second Isaiah and the
book of Jonah is sometimes drawn upon by New Testament writers
for a description, explanation, and glorification of Jesus' function.

23. At this place it ought to be recalled that the statements made
by Jesus, Stephen, and Paul concerning the hardening of the hearts
of the Jews (Mark 4:1-12, Matt. 19:8, 23:37; Rom. 9-11; 1 Thess. 2:15;
Acts 7, 13:46-47, 28:25-28) come from Jews and are in the best of Prophetic tradition. There is nothing anti-Semitic in a Jew's chiding his
brothers for their disobedience to God. But the New Testament gives
no evidence—except in the allusion to the Jonah story and to the last
judgment (Matt. 12:41-42, Luke 11:31-32; cf. Rom. 2:14-16)—of Gentiles
sitting in judgment over the Jews. *Quod licet Jovi, non licet bovi.*

24. This contest is beautifully illustrated by the fable of the ring
and the three brothers in G. E. Lessing's *Nathan der Weise.*

25. In this I agree with Paul Tillich; see "The Theology of Missions," *op. cit.*, p. 38.

26. A recent approach to some of the pertinent problems and
biographical help is offered, for example, by the article *pisteuo* by
Arthur Weiser and Rudolf Bultmann, in *Theologisches Wörterbuch
zum Neuen Testament*, ed. Gerhard Kittel (Stuttgart: W. Kohlhammer,
VI, 1959), pp. 174-230. English translation by D. H. Barton, P. R.
Ackroyd, A. E. Harvey in *Bible Key Words* III (New York: Harper &
Brothers, 1961).

27. Rom. 9:31-32; cf. the context 9:30—10:21; also Gal. 2:16-17,
3:19-25; Phil. 3:2-11; 2 Cor. 3:4-18.

28. As especially H. J. Schoeps has attempted to prove, in *Paul.*

29. The last part of Martin Noth's otherwise excellent essay on
"The Laws in the Pentateuch" in *The Laws in the Pentateuch and
Other Studies*, trans. D. R. Ap-Thomas (Philadelphia: The Westminster
Press, 1961; also London: Oliver and Boyd, 1966), may be mentioned
as an example.

30. These individuals are frequently identified simply by the word "some" (Greek: *tines*), for example, in Acts 15:1, 5, 24; Galatians 1:7, 2:12; cf. 5:10. They are also called "false brethren secretly brought in" (Gal. 2:4). Johannes Munck, *Paul and the Salvation of Mankind* (Richmond: John Knox Press, 1959), says that Paul's Galatian opponents were Gentile Christians emulating what they considered the ways of true Jews; 2 Corinthians 11:22, Galatians 2:12-13, Acts 21:27 describe Paul's opponents as Jews coming from Jerusalem or Asia Minor. It is probable that among both Judaeo- and Gentile Christians Paul's message was twisted. Munck has helped to free the Jews from the charge that they alone sought to supplement the gospel by specific legalistic additions.

31. See the Rosenzweig quotations on the Strassburg figures cited in H. J. Schoeps, *The Jewish-Christian Argument,* p. 143, and Buber's self-identification with "all the ashes, all the ruin, all the wordless misery" and his reference to Yebamot 47a, cited by Schoeps, p. 157.

32. If passages such as Galatians 2:16, 20; 3:26; Romans 3:22, 25, 26; Philippians 3:9 are understood in the light of statements concerning Jesus' obedience, it becomes clear that not only faith *in* the Messiah but Jesus' the Messiah's own faith is meant, when Paul speaks of "justification by faith." The epistle to the Hebrews (especially 2:17 —3:6, 12:2) puts specific stress on Jesus' faith.

33. In Chicago in the spring of 1962, Karl Barth, to the surprise and joy of a group of Jewish scholars, answered with a plain "yes" the question: "Do you think a faithful Jew may please God as much as a faithful Christian?" Karl Barth argued on the following line: Since Jesus said Abraham rejoiced that he was to see his (Jesus') day (John 8:56), any son of Abraham who is looking forward to the coming of the Messiah shares Abraham's faith. It was this faith which made Abraham find favor with God. ". . . those who are men of faith are blessed with Abraham who had faith" (Gal. 3:9).

34. Martin Buber in a monograph under this title. The following distinctions are gleaned from books or essays of Leo Baeck, Franz Rosenzweig, Eugen Rosenstock-Huessy, J. W. Parkes, Will Herberg, H. J. Schoeps, Reinhold Mayer. We refer only to benevolent distinctions and omit all those that appear to reveal a patent or latent Marcionite, anti-Semitic, idealistic, antinomian, anti-ceremonial, or atheistic bias. For this reason the medieval description of the Jews as perfidious, accursed murderers of God; the blasts of Luther against the Jews (in 1543, caused as they were by his disappointment that they did not convert to the Reformation; cf. his 1523 essay on Jesus, the Jew), the idealists' (especially Hegel's) depreciatory remarks against the Jews and the subsequent writing of early church history; finally modern polemics uttered on the lines of the *Deutsche Christen,* will not be taken into consideration. They are a sin and a shame on the shield of the churches that call themselves Christian. It is a relief to note that at the Second Vatican Council a Schema was adopted which opens at least an avenue toward redress.

35. Steven Schwarzschild, "Judaism, Scripture, and Ecumenism,"

op. cit., p. 131, quotes Maimonides' (unexpurgated!) *Mishne Torah* XI 4; in H. J. Schoeps, *op. cit.,* pp. 109 and 141-142, references to Formstecher and Rosenzweig are made.

36. According to 1 Corinthians 12:13, Colossians 3:11, Galatians 3:28 (cf. Ephesians 2:11-22 and 5:20—6:9), the removal of the Jewish-Gentile segregation and discrimination precedes, illustrates, and entails the unity overcoming all other separations.

CHAPTER II

1. Justin, *Dialogue with Trypho;* H. Hailperin, *Rashi and the Christian Scholars* (Pittsburgh: University of Pittsburgh Press, 1963); John Lightfoot, *Horae Hebraicae et Talmudicae* (Leipzig: F. Lanckisius, 1675); Strack-Billerbeck, *op. cit.;* Adolf Schlatter, *Der Evangelist Matthäus* (Stuttgart: Calwer Vereinsbuchhandlung, 1933); Gerhard Kittel and Gerhard Friedrich, *Theological Dictionary of the New Testament,* trans. G. W. Bromiley (Grand Rapids: W. B. Eerdmans, 1964-).

2. I-III (Cambridge: Harvard University Press, seventh ed., 1954).

3. *Theology of the New Testament,* Vol. I, pp. 164-183.

4. E.g., W. Heitmüller; Adolf Deissmann; Hans Lietzmann; Albert Schweitzer; Ernst Käsemann in his earlier writings.

5. Especially by W. D. Davies, *Paul and Rabbinic Judaism* (London: S.P.C.K., 1948); Schoeps, *Paul;* C. K. Bennett, *From First Adam to Last* (New York: Charles Scribner's Sons, 1962).

6. *Vorrede zum Römerbrief,* 1522 and 1546, Weimar ed., Deutsche Bibel VI (Weimar: H. Böhlaus Nachfolger, 1931), pp. 26-27.

7. E.g., Alfred Jepsen, "Zedeq und Zedaqah im Alten Testament," *Gottes Wort und Gottes Land,* Festschrift für H.-W. Hertzberg, ed. H. Reventlow (Göttingen: Vandenhoeck und Ruprecht, 1965), pp. 78-89; Peter Stuhlmacher, *Gerechtigkeit Gottes bei Paulus* (Göttingen: Vandenhoeck und Ruprecht, 1965).

8. E.g., Gal. 4:4; Phil. 2:6-8; Rom. 5:18-19, 8:4.

9. E.g., Rom. 8:4; Gal. 3:13, 4:4, 5:14, 6:2; Phil. 2:1-8.

10. See Romans 8:2; Galatians 3:13, 3:19, 4:8-10.

11. As in Heb. 5:12, Eph. 2:14, Col. 2:8.

12. Hab. 2:4, in Gal. 3:11 ff.; Rom. 1:17, 10:5 ff.; Gal. 2:20, 6:2; cf. Ragnar Bring's interpretation of the use Paul makes of Lev. 18:5, *Commentary on Galatians,* trans. Eric Wahlstrom (Philadelphia: Muhlenberg Press, 1961), pp. 130-142; C. E. B. Cranfield, "St. Paul and the Law," *Scottish Journal of Theology,* 17, 1964, pp. 43-68, esp. pp. 49-50.

13. Gal. 5:3, 6:13; cf. Rom. 2:25.

14. Gal. 6:13; cf. Munck, *op. cit.,* ch. IV.

15. Such as 1 Cor. 9:20-21; Acts 16:3-4, 21:24-26.

16. Gal. 3:15-18; Rom. 4:9-18.

17. Rom. 2:12, 21-24; 3:19-20.

18. Schoeps, *Paul,* pp. 28-32, 197-200, 213-218.

19. But see, for example, G. S. Duncan's interpretation of Galatians 3:19, *The Epistle of Paul to the Galatians,* Moffat New Testament

Commentary (London: Hodder and Stoughton, eighth reprint, 1955),
pp. 111-115.
20. Davies, *op. cit.*
21. Gal. 2:10; 2 Cor. 8-9; Acts 11:27-30.
22. Gal. 2:12; Acts 15:1, 5; 2 Cor. 11:13, 22; Phil. 3:2.
23. Gal. 1:15-16, 2:1; 2 Cor. 12:1-4; Acts 16:9-10, 18:9-10; etc.
24. E.g., 1 Cor. 1:23, 2:2, 15:4-58.
25. Just as Pss. 69:23-29, 109:6-20, 137:7-9.
26. Cf. F. C. Grant, *Ancient Judaism and the New Testament*
(New York: The Macmillan Company, 1959), p. 14.
27. As in Luke 23:34a; Acts 23:5; 1 Tim. 1:13.
28. Eph. 4:4-6; cf. Gal. 3:27-28, Rom. 10:9-15.
29. 1 Thess. 4:13 ff.; 2 Thess. 1:7 ff.; Phil. 4:5; Col. 3:4; Rom. 8:19.
30. *Paul and His Interpreters,* trans. W. Montgomery (London:
A. and C. Black, 1950).
31. In his later writings.
32. As in Rom. 3:21; Eph. 2:13; 2 Cor. 6:2.
33. 1 Cor. 10:11; Gal. 1:4, 6:15; 2 Cor. 5:17; Col. 1:13.
34. Gal. 1:22-24; 2 Cor. 3:1-3.
35. In 1 and 2 Thess., Gal. 6:7-10, Rom. 2:5-13, 1 Cor. 3:12-15,
2 Cor. 5:10, etc.
36. Bring, *op. cit.,* especially pp. 130, 241, 275 ff.; Kurt Stalder,
Das Werk des Geistes in der Heiligung bei Paulus (Zürich: EVZ-Verlag,
1962), especially pp. 455 ff., 464 f.; Eberhard Jüngel, *Paulus und Jesus*
(Tübingen: J. C. B. Mohr, second ed., 1964), especially pp. 66-70.

CHAPTER III

1. *Die Probleme der Kolosser- und Epheserbriefe* (Lund: C. W. K.
Gleerup, 1946); see also Heinrich Schlier, *Der Brief an die Epheser*
(Düsseldorf: Patmos-Verlag, 1958).
2. E.g., Rom. 8:35 ff.
3. A full bibliography for the study of Ephesians and its specific
problems and also an extensive discussion of dissonant and harmonious
scholarly interpretations will be found in the author's commentary
on Ephesians in the Anchor Bible.
4. Eph. 2:12, 19-22; 4:15-16; 5:24-32.
5. Eph. 1:17 ff.; 3:10, 18 f.
6. Eph. 1:9, 15 f.; 2:7; 3:1—6:20
7. Eph. 1:6, 12, 14; 3:21; 5:27.
8. Eph. 1:5, 6, 15; 2:4; 3:17, 19; 4:2-3; 5:1 f., 25-33; 6:23 f.
9. Eph. 2:11, 17; cf. 2:1 ff., 4:17 ff.
10. E.g., 1 Thess. 2:14-16; Gal. 3:7-29, 4:21-31, 6:16; 1 Cor. 10:18;
Rom. 2:28 f.; 9-11, and particularly Rom. 9:6, Phil. 3:2 f.
11. Unless otherwise noted, in this section the following translations
from Ephesians are the author's.
12. Cf. 2:20, 3:13, 4:1, 11, 6:19-20.
13. Cf. Col. 3:11, 1 Cor. 12:13.
14. Eph. 5:21—6:9, Col. 3:18—4:1.

15. 1 Cor. 12:13; Eph. 1:22, 3:6, 4:4 and 15 f., 5:23 and 30.
16. Rom. 1:16-17, 2:9 f., 3:9 and 29; Acts 13:5, 46 ff., etc.
17. Eph. 5:1 f., 8, 21; 6:23.
18. Cf. Heb. 11; Gal. 3; Rom. 4.
19. Matt. 10:2-6, 19:28, 26:26-29; John 6:66-71.
20. John 1:47; cf. 4:23 f.; Rom. 2:28 f.
21. Gal. 3:10 f., 4:21 ff.; Phil. 3:2-9; 2 Cor. 10 ff.; Rom. 10:2-3.
22. Cf. 1 Cor. 10:16 f., 11:24 f.; Heb. 9:12-14; John 6:53-56, 63.
23. In Eph. 1:3-14, 2:12, 3:1-11.
24. Eph. 4:6, Rom. 3:30, 1 Cor. 8:6.
25. Cf. Rom. 1:2, 3:21; 2 Cor. 3:4-18; Gal. 3-4; Heb. 1:1; 1 Peter
1:10-11; Matt. 5:17.
26. Acts 9:1-16, 22:6-15, 26:12-18; Gal. 1:16.
27. See 2:20-22; 3:17; 4:1, 15-17, 25, 28; 6:11, 13-14.